DEBRETT'S GUIDE TO SPEAKING IN PUBLIC

Also by Carole McKenzie

Presenting for Women in Business
Successful Presentations
Perfect Stress Control
Quotable Women
Quotable Sex
Quotable Royalty
Quotable Politicians
Quotable Vices

DEBRETT'S GUIDE TO SPEAKING IN PUBLIC

How to prepare and deliver speeches
and toasts for all occasions

Carole McKenzie

HEADLINE

My special thanks to DQ for her help and technical skills

First published in 1994
by HEADLINE BOOK PUBLISHING

Reprinted in this edition in 1994
by HEADLINE BOOK PUBLISHING

10 9 8 7 6 5 4 3 2 1

British Library Cataloguing in Publication Data

McKenzie, Carole
  Debrett's Guide to Speaking in Public
  New ed
  I. Title
  808.51

  ISBN 0–7472–1007–1

Typeset by
Letterpart Limited, Reigate, Surrey

Printed and bound in Great Britain by
Mackays of Chatham PLC, Chatham, Kent

HEADLINE BOOK PUBLISHING
A division of Hodder Headline PLC
338 Euston Road
London NW1 3BH

To My Father
With Love

Contents

Introduction 1

Preparing a Speech: General Advice 7

What Are Your Objectives? 8
Audience Profile 10
Brevity and Simplicity 11

Preparing a Speech: Instructions in Detail 13

Structure 13
The Opening 14
The Body 18
The Summary 20

Drafting and Scripting 22

General Advice 22
Text Layout 23
Marking Your Script 25
Visual Aids and Cues 25
The Teleprompter (Autocue) 30

Keeping Audience Interest: General Advice 32

Quotations 32
Visual Aids 32
Using Humour 40

Body Language 41

General Advice 41

Posture 43
Gesture 45
Expression 45
Hands 45
Positive Attitude 47

First Impressions 48

Dress 48
Developing Your Own Style 50
Appearance and Body Language Checklist 52

Controlling Nerves 54

Timing and Editing 58

Timing 58
Editing 58

Delivery 60

Your Voice 60
Communication checklist 61
Verbal Communication 62
Pronunciation 66
Using the Microphone 69
The Media 72

Preparation Summaries 76

Social Toasts and Speeches 80

The Loyal Toast 80
Grace 80
Toast to the Ladies 81

Wedding Speeches — 84

General Advice — 84
Planning Checklist — 86
The Father of the Bride — 88
The Groom — 89
The Best Man — 90
Adapting Jokes — 90
Toast to Absent Friends — 90
Sample Speeches — 91

Anniversary and Birthday Toasts — 105

Wedding Anniversary — 105
Birthday Celebrations — 106
Sample Speeches — 107

Christenings — 114

After-dinner Speaking — 117

General Advice — 117
Research — 119
After-dinner Humour — 122
Stance — 124
Full After-dinner Speech Sample — 125
Summary — 131

Presentation of Awards — 134

General Advice — 134
The School — 135
Sample Speeches — 135

Political and Business — 138

Political — 138
Business — 140

Sporting Toasts   142

General Advice   142
Sample Speeches   142

The Role of the Chairman   149

General Advice   149
The Speakers   152
Other Roles of the Chairman   154

Booking and Briefing Speakers   161

Any Questions?   164

General Advice   164

Other Types of Speaking Situations   177

Impromptu Speaking   177
Extemporaneous Speaking   178
The Lecture   178
The Technical Presentation   181
Talks to Foreign Groups   182
Bar Mitzvah   183
University Graduation Party   183
Visiting Delegations   184
Funerals   184
Competitive Presentations   185

Correct Form   188

Useful Quips and Quotations   194

General Advice   194

Hamlet's Advice   204

He rose without a friend and sat down without an enemy.

Henry Grattan

How many grave speeches which have surprised, shocked and directed the nation, have been made by Great Men too soon after a noble dinner, words winged by the Press without an accompanying and explanatory wine list.

H.L.M. Tomlinson

I do not object to people looking at their watches when I am speaking. But I strongly object when they start shaking them to make certain they are still going.

Lord Birkett

He Hears
On all sides, from innumerable tongues,
A dismal universal hiss, the sound
Of public scorn.

John Milton

You know very well that after a certain age a man has only one speech.

George Bernard Shaw

Why doesn't the fellow who says, 'I'm no speechmaker', let it go at that instead of giving a demonstration.

F. McKinney

Introduction

As an author of several books on Quotations, I would like to start with one of my favourite quotations about making speeches.

> If your face is not clean, wash it: don't throw it away and cut your head off. If your diction is slipshod and impure, correct and purify it: don't throw it away and make shift for the rest of your life with a hideous affectation accent, false emphases, unmeaning pauses, aggravating slowness, ill-conditioned gravity, and perverse resolution to 'get it from the chest' and make it sound as if you got it from the cellar. Of course, if you are a professional humbug – a bishop or a judge, for instance – then the case is different; for the salary makes it seem worth your while to dehumanise yourself and pretend to belong to a different species.
>
> George Bernard Shaw (1856–1950)

A speech is like a love affair. Most successful when entered into with enthusiasm and commitment from both parties; in this case the speaker and the audience. The interaction between the two will provide you with the ingredients for success.

I believe that one of the key elements of a successful speech is the element of being oneself. When giving speeches it is tempting, particularly for the beginner, to 'adopt' a particular style. Often they have witnessed this style working successfully for a particular presenter and believe that they also can make it work for them. This is seldom the case. The difference between a mediocre performance and a memorable one is the element of personality. Each of us has our own unique style. No two presenters will deliver a speech in the same manner.

All good speeches adhere to the general guidelines outlined

in this book. The factor which makes the difference is the ability to be yourself and let your enjoyment show. If you can also inject some humour, you will have all the ingredients to make memorable speeches.

What Makes This Book Different From Others on the Market?
Many books on public speaking make a definite distinction between the different types of speaking occasions. These tend to be divided up into Business and Social (usually under the heading of After-dinner/Wedding speeches). This often means that you need to research two different types of book to obtain your information.

Whether you have to give a speech, informal talk, toast, or a more formal business presentation, the same general guidelines apply. This book contains examples and advice for *all* of these occasions.

What Makes a Good Speaker?

There is just no way around it – you have to do your homework. A speaker may be very well informed, but if he hasn't thought out exactly what he wants to say *today, to this audience*, he has no business taking up other people's valuable time.

Iococca: An Autobiography

Television provides us with perfect images, of speeches where nothing goes wrong, where it all looks effortless and easy. This is not the case; these perfect speeches, witty, sharp and to the point are the result of hours of work. Often teams of professional scriptwriters have been at work behind the scenes, and speakers are professionally groomed and dressed for the occasion. It is well to remember that behind every professional speech is a series of out-takes, moments when speakers have forgotten their words, lost their notes, or been struck dumb with fright.

Don't be afraid to admit to yourself that the whole idea of public speaking is frightening. This is natural. If professionals feel this way about making speeches, then you are certainly entitled to feel the same.

When speakers are asked why they feel nervous about speaking in public, their answers generally fall under the following areas:

- Fear of saying or doing something that will make them look foolish.
- Fear and discomfort at revealing something personal about themselves to strangers.
- Lack of self-confidence. Particularly if this is their first speech-making occasion.

Most of these fears are irrational and can be eliminated if you organise well, and remember that the main element which will help you deliver a successful speech is THOROUGH PREPARATION.

Thorough preparation is the key to a professional performance, but there are two other important elements which will hasten your success as a speaker.

SINCERITY

This is an essential element for the public speaker. If you set yourself up to be something you are not, for example, 'an expert' in a particular topic, your audience will quickly catch on and spot the fake. What often results, is that the audience will set itself to expose you. The audience can sense sincerity in a speaker. It's the enthusiasm and passion that accompanies his words and actions, and a feeling of genuine interest in them and their concerns. A good speaker also believes in the value of his message. His obvious preparation and careful handling of the subject signals to them that the occasion and subject are worthy of his time and effort.

This level of professionalism and sincerity will help the speaker forge a link with his audience. The audience will respect these attributes, and will happily hear him out and will him to succeed.

INTRODUCTION

Sincerity is quickly spotted by the audience, but the style of delivery can also make or break a good speech.

CONVERSATION

Some of the best speeches I have heard have all included this element. The speaker, instead of treating the audience as a 'whole', has treated them as individuals; including them by using positive body language, humour, rapport, and making them feel that they are part of the occasion.

This style is relevant for all occasions, but particularly for celebratory events such as marriage speeches. Guests from both families will perhaps be meeting together for the first time. The speaker's approach and style can set the tone for the occasion, and allow the guests to share in the happy event.

- A professional approach towards your material and your audience will gain you their respect and admiration.
- Being true to yourself, emphasising your positive attributes, and showing how your knowledge and strengths can help the audience, will help build credibility and sincerity.
- Treating the audience as individuals will forge a bond and form a rapport, which will help you fulfil your speech objectives.
- Show enthusiasm. A positive approach is uplifting and welcome to the audience. They would rather listen to an interesting and enthusiastic voice than a speech delivered in a boring monotone. Using positive words and phrases will help keep your speech upbeat.
- Use language which matches the occasion.

Professor Rosabeth Moss Kanter, an American communications expert and excellent public speaker sums up these qualities:

The first and most fundamental skill of a good speaker is to be an expert and to *know your subject well*.

The second important skill is *self-confidence*; to recover quickly from mistakes and even make a joke out of them; and

4

to be flexible enough to bring in new material spontaneously or make changes on the spot.

The third key is to *empathise* with the audience. It is important that their needs be met and that the emotional state of the audience be kept first and foremost in the speaker's mind. It is up to the speaker to relax a tense audience with a joke, to reassure people that the difficult subjects will be handled well and to:

> *treat members of the audience as individuals*
> *who are potential friends and supporters.*

I particularly like this last piece of advice, and many experienced speakers would agree. If you do your preparation, whether you are speaking at a formal or informal occasion, adopt a positive attitude, and be determined to enjoy yourself, then you have a recipe for success. Your audience are willing you to succeed, indeed they will often go out of their way to help you do this. And, if some little thing does not go to plan, they will forgive you.

That is why we enjoy watching out-takes of familiar television programmes, particularly when the bloomers are made by television personalities who are normally presented as being super cool and professional. It reminds us that public speaking is not easy, it takes lots of hard work and practice; but the finished result is well worth the effort.

Everyone dreads the thought of speaking in public. One public speaker started his after-dinner speech with the following anecdote, saying that he was suffering from the Androcles effect:

Androcles faced the most terrifying of man-eating lions ever to enter an ancient Roman Colosseum, but the gentle fellow had a way of taming the ferocious beast. He simply whispered into its ear and it abandoned all thought of eating him. Summoned to the royal box, Androcles was asked his secret by the emperor.

'It's this, my lord. I merely tell the lion that, as soon as he's finished dinner, he'll be asked to just say a few words.'

INTRODUCTION

If you have heard that whisper, I hope that you will read and enjoy this book.

How to Use This Book
The general guidelines on preparation, structure and delivery are relevant to all speaking occasions. Specific advice on particular areas can be found under the relevant subject heading.

You may find that in place of the word 'speech', I use the words 'talk' or 'presentation', presentation being more often used to describe business speaking occasions.

Today, with the blurring of boundaries between professional and social life, all are relevant and have come to mean the same thing. All mean a 'sharing' with the audience. A sharing of self, of ideas, knowledge, emotions and information with other people. Perhaps a more appropriate word would be *'conversation'*.

Finally, increasing numbers of excellent public speakers are women. Please therefore read 'he' as 'he/she'.

Preparing a Speech: General Advice

90% preparation – 10% perspiration

Quite often the most difficult aspect of making a speech is getting started, and procrastination is common. False starts, mental blocks, general lack of motivation and feelings of panic, are just some of the excuses for not getting down to it. You will find that once you do make a start, the rest of your preparation will follow on. Here are some ideas to get you started:

Lack of Facts
If you are not sure that you have all the facts, you naturally hesitate to start planning your speech.

Do some more research. Collect relevant quotations, anecdotes, interesting facts which you think may be useful. If, for example, you are asked to give a speech to a retiring employee, then speak to their colleagues. They will have a fund of stories and incidents which may be helpful.

Fact File
For future reference, keep a fact file. Photocopy research information, newspaper clippings, journal articles. Often, company newsletters and bulletins contain a wealth of interesting information about company personnel, and specific departments. The Personnel Department can also supply information such as employee start date, any special awards, etc. This file will prove a useful resource for future reference.

Lack of Starting Point
When you have collected your information, it can be quite a

daunting task to sit down and put it all together. Use the salami technique, i.e. break it up into manageable areas. For example if your speech is not imminent, you could ease yourself into it by perhaps starting to work on the objectives or the audience profile. By working on it, small steps at a time, you will soon complete the preparation.

Lack of Creativity

Creative thinking helps when preparing a speech and cannot be forced. Often working on your speech when you are at your best helps. If you work best in the morning, then set some time aside to outline ideas.

If you must prepare at your workplace, ensure that you are not disturbed. Try brainstorming; this will enable you to evaluate the information and include what is relevant for the particular occasion.

TO BRAINSTORM

Jot down broad ideas on your topic as you think of them. Don't try to organise them at this stage. When you have exhausted your ideas, look at them again and see if you can link them together. Look for patterns. Do the ideas fall into general areas?

Preparation

There are three important questions which should be answered before you progress with your preparation. The first is:

WHAT ARE YOUR OBJECTIVES?

What are you trying to achieve? Are you attempting to inform, persuade, motivate, or entertain the audience? Objectives for making a wedding speech or proposing a toast are evident, but for many other types of speeches you must be quite clear what the objective is. This information forms the basis of your preparation. For example, your objective may be:

- To motivate staff to improve customer service.
- To inform the Parent–Teacher Association of the latest computer packages.
- To persuade the Golf Club committee to adopt electronic identity cards for members.
- To entertain an audience of business people at an after-dinner function.
- To present prizes on Speech Day.

Try to state your objective in a sentence. Write it on a card and place it in front of you as you work through the preparation.

Decide what information is important for the particular audience you are speaking to. For example if you are talking to the PTA about computer packages, you would need to know what the equipment will be used for, how much the school is prepared to pay, and most importantly, how much time you have to put your case across. You would then perhaps want to include a demonstration as part of your talk, as well as show samples of work.

Each group will require slightly different treatment, but the general guidelines in this section are appropriate for all speeches. When you are clear about your objectives, you must now think about your audience. The more you know about them, the better you will be able to construct a speech which will be both meaningful and interesting. Often it is possible to obtain a list from your host before the event; this information will usually show names, titles and companies of those present. If you are to make a wedding speech, it would be useful to have a copy of the guest list.

You can then highlight names of those you wish to give special mention. The following is a suggested Audience Profile. It is by no means exhaustive, but will give you some idea of the sort of questions you may want answered. It will serve as a starting point for your preparation. Use this as a basic model; it will help you compile your own list.

PREPARING A SPEECH: GENERAL ADVICE

AUDIENCE PROFILE

FOR GENERAL BUSINESS AND AFTER-DINNER EVENTS

- Who do they represent (company, organisation)?
- What are their job titles, responsibilities, backgrounds, levels of knowledge, education, ages?
- Is it a mixed audience or all male/female?
- Is it a multi-racial audience?
- How technical will the talk be?
- Is there a political factor involved?
- What is the likely mood of the audience, receptive or hostile?
- What approach should I take, formal or informal?
- What are their objectives?
- What's in it for them, i.e. what's the hook?
- What do I expect from them in the way of response or action?
- How many people will attend?
- Other.

WEDDINGS (e.g. best man's speech)

- Seating arrangements. Who is at the top table?
- Names of all those who will be mentioned in the speech (e.g. bridesmaids).
- How many guests will attend?
- Special welcomes (e.g. relatives who have travelled from Australia to attend, relatives recovering from illness etc).
- People who have contributed to the day (vicar, caterers, hotel staff).

Audience Size and Room Layout

It is always useful for a speaker to have a look at the room where the speech will take place. This is not always possible, particularly for the client-type presentation, as these often take place on client premises.

Other occasions, such as after-dinner and wedding speeches benefit here, as they usually take place in hotels with easy access.

There are no hard and fast rules about room layout, except

that the audience must be able to:

- *See* and *hear* the speaker clearly.
- If it is a small group you will not need a microphone, but this is useful if speaking to large groups. Most wedding speeches are delivered without the use of a microphone, often to up to a hundred guests.
- *Be comfortable* for the length of time they will be sitting. For example, check that the room is the correct temperature, and if it is a large group, that there is sufficient ventilation.

If it is a small audience in a large room, *arrange* for the group to occupy seating towards the front of the room, rather than have them scattered. This will *ease communication*.

Alternative Approach
Let us consider what to do if you have insufficient time/ information to produce an audience profile.

Often refreshments are served before the speakers take the stage. In this case, use the time to circulate and speak to as many people as you can.

Wedding speeches have an advantage here as the key speakers will have ample opportunity to circulate amongst the guests. The main advantage in being able to make contact with your audience before the speech is quite simply that you won't be standing up 'cold'. Seeing a few familiar faces before you will help reduce nerves. If you have also exchanged a few words with them beforehand, then when you speak it will be like speaking to familiar friends.

BREVITY AND SIMPLICITY

One of the key mistakes that people make when preparing a toast, a few words of opening for a Christmas fete, or a prize-giving address, is to ask 'What do they usually say at these events?' Avoid clichés, copy-cat addresses, and material that doesn't match your speaking style. *Your aim should be to deliver a speech which is custom-made for the particular event, individuals, and organisations involved.*

When you are invited to give a speech, you will usually be given some idea of timing. Most after-dinner and business speeches will be around thirty minutes long. You may have been asked to speak because you are a specialist in your field of business, or are an enthusiast who knows a lot about a particular subject. Most people who know their subject well are enthusiastic about it, and want to share their knowledge and expertise with others.

This can often lead to long speeches which lose their punch and interest halfway through. Be brief. It is rare to hear an audience complain about a speech being too short, but common to see an audience who are bored and uninterested with a speaker who has long outstayed his welcome.

I recommend that if you are given, say, fifteen minutes to deliver a speech, then you work within this limit, aiming for slightly less, say twelve minutes. Keep it short and punchy. In the business speech, if you are the only speaker, you may wish to speak for twenty minutes and take ten minutes of questions. Question time is always welcomed by the audience, particularly if the subject is interesting, controversial and affects them personally.

Keep it simple. Don't use long words if you know shorter ones. When writing out your notes stick to short sentences as this will enable you to make good use of the pause, and also allow you to breathe. If we think of a speech as being a one-to-one conversation with your audience, then a good rule of thumb is to use conversational words. Avoid clichés, jargon, slang, and swear words.

In this age of computers, it is often difficult to avoid using jargon. If it is unavoidable, for example if you are giving a technical speech, try to briefly explain what the jargon means. Never assume that your audience has heard it before.

Even the mildest swear words should be avoided as they may give offence.

Preparing a Speech: Instructions in Detail

*A well-prepared speech is already
nine-tenths delivered.*

STRUCTURE

Every speech needs some kind of structure or organisation. Often a potentially good speech falls down because this element is missing.

Structure in this context means the organisational blueprint for your speech.

All speeches may be conveniently divided into three main areas: The *Opening*, The *Body*, and the *Close*. They can be summarised as follows:

THE OPENING
Tell them [the audience] what you are going to tell them.

THE BODY
Tell them.

THE CLOSE
Tell them what you told them.

This formula works for most speaking occasions. Television newsreaders are familiar with this formula. They open with a punchy headline, often accompanied by dramatic visuals – this gains the attention of their audience.

13

PREPARING A SPEECH: INSTRUCTIONS IN DETAIL

They then go into detail, developing the theme, then finish with a summing up and close. If, for example you think of an after-dinner speech, this formula works well. Starting with the opening – an attention grabber, then building up the theme with anecdotes, humour, and ending with a punch line, which pulls the whole speech together.

The time spent on each section will vary, but as a general rule and for maximum impact, spend around:

15% of your total time available on the Opening

75% on the Body, and

10% on the Close.

The first and last sentences of any speech are crucial. The importance of a clear and resounding first sentence and a well-rounded finale cannot be over-emphasised. You must capture the attention of your audience at the beginning, keep them interested throughout the body and leave them satisfied at the end.

THE OPENING

The purpose of the Opening of the speech is to hook the attention of the audience. It is the first few words spoken to the audience by way of an introduction to yourself and your topic. When you stand up to begin your speech:

- Pause and look at the audience (this will alert them to the fact that you are about to begin).
- Smile, providing it is not a serious topic.
- Choose the opening that is appropriate for the audience and the presentation objectives.

The opening of a speech is crucial. Making a good start to your speech will give you confidence and help reduce your nerves.

PREPARING A SPEECH: INSTRUCTIONS IN DETAIL

Recent research shows that an audience remembers the opening and closing remarks of a speech more readily than the rest.

There are a variety of ways to open a speech. Here are a few examples:

ANECDOTE
For example, the story about Androcles (see page 5). This is a good ice-breaker as it begins with humour. Also the audience empathises with the speaker's feelings about being nervous.

QUOTATION
If you use this method, make sure that the quotation is relevant to your topic. I often quote Robert Burns to introduce and explain to students the benefits of using video in training.

> O wad some pow'r the giftie gi'e us
> To see ourselves as ithers see us
> It wad frae mony a blunder free us
> An' foolish notion.

This of course, refers to feedback, an essential ingredient of good communication.

LITERARY DEVICES
These are very good introductory means of reinforcement. Metaphors, slogans, unique language, literary description, are all possible ways to get the needed early impact. Note: Don't over-dramatise or appear affected.

ACHIEVEMENTS AND TRADITIONS
These can be good historical starters. They refer respectively to success achieved by members of the audience or others whom they respect. Note: Avoid flattery. Praise must always be sincere.

HISTORICAL FACTS
Use relevant events that tie in with the date of the speech. For example the following all took place on 4 January:

15

1919: 'The Ministry of Food are able to confirm that all food rationing will end in April.' (This could be used, for example, in speeches to do with food, e.g. food retailers.)

1950: 'Sir Frederick Bell, chairman of the Scottish Herring Industry Board believes kippers could be a big dollar earner this year.' (Audiences with interest in fishing, angling, marketing.)

1966: 'The price of runaway romance went up 100% today. Registrar's fees went up from 11s 3d to 28s plus cost of intimation.' (Weddings, expense etc.)

Several newspapers include a section on historical dates/events from the world of sport, politics and business. Collect these for your fact file. Here is one from my local Edinburgh newspaper to bring in the New Year:

1896: 'The advent of the New Year occasioned the usual scenes of low-class hilarity at the Tron Church.'

OTHER DEVICES

- Show how subject can affect the audience.
- Use an exhibit/model/visual.
- Make a direct statement.
- Pose the problem.
- Invite audience participation.

The Introduction
Depending on the type of speech you are giving, there are certain elements which you should include in the introduction. Some elements will vary. For example the following should be included in the more formal type of presentation/ lecture, where the audience have not met you before.

- The first thing is to get the audience's attention. A good **opener** should achieve this. Smile and give your audience a

16

warm welcome. Remember to look as if you are happy to be with them.

- Early on in the introduction tell the audience a bit about yourself. Keep it brief and relevant, e.g. name, job, credentials.
- Remember the Opening – 'Tell them what you are going to tell them.' Therefore, introduce the topic title and say how you are going to cover the subject. For example:

I have been asked along today to speak about Graphology (handwriting analysis).

First I'll begin by telling you about the *history* of graphology.

Next we'll look at some of the *principles* used in graphological analysis.

Finally, we'll see how graphology can be used as an *aid to staff recruitment*.

You can see that the topic has been divided into three areas. When you have decided on your subject, always break it down into three (a maximum of four areas). This will help you to keep the information to manageable proportions. This can now be used as the 'skeleton' for your speech, and in fact provides you with an agenda.

For example, the above could be displayed on a flipchart (for a small group), or on an overhead or 35mm slide, as follows:

GRAPHOLOGY

- The history of Graphology.
- General principles.
- Graphology as an aid to Recruitment.

When you have told the audience about yourself and how you are going to tackle the subject and in what order, there are a few other things which they may need to know.

If relevant:

- Tell them *how long* the speech will last.

- *Set the ground rules for questions*, i.e. 'Please stop me at any time if you have a question.' Or, 'Please keep your questions until the end.' A general rule here: It is easier for the speaker not to have interruptions during his speech. The speech will flow better; also timing will be more accurate. If you have a choice this order may suit the new or relatively inexperienced speaker. However, some topics – technical talks, or speeches involving statistics, or controversial material – are better handled where questions are not saved until the end. In this case, if you have, say, three areas, as in the Graphology example, questions could be invited after each section. This will help break up the text, and help add interest and participation from the audience.
- State your *objectives*.
  Think about the type of talk you are giving, e.g. informative, motivational, persuasive. Tell the audience why you are giving the talk.
- Tell them if you have **supporting material** to give them (this could be handouts, brochures, examples, reports).
  Providing that the audience do not need this material during the speech, then tell them they will get it at the end. There is nothing more infuriating than to sit through a speech taking notes, only to be told at the end that you will receive a copy of the whole speech.
  Example: 'Copies of the report will be given out at the end of question time, so unless you particularly want to, there is no need to take notes'.
- Always **make a clear link** between the Opening, Body and Close. In this case, a simple link into the Body of the talk might be: Let's start with – the History of Graphology.

THE BODY

All speech written or spoken is a dead language until it finds a willing and prepared hearer.

Robert Louis Stevenson

PREPARING A SPEECH: INSTRUCTIONS IN DETAIL

You have now hooked the attention of your audience, and made your introductions. The Body follows on from your introduction, and you should aim to keep up the level of interest attained in your opening remarks.

The Body should follow a logical sequence with frequent signposting, leading the audience through the talk towards the objectives. Research shows that the attention span of the audience varies at different times of the day: for example, high attention levels at the beginning of the day, after coffee; and low before breaks, after lunch and late afternoon. Often you will not have a choice of speaking time, but on most occasions speeches take place after or during coffee, i.e. after-dinner, wedding speeches, and conference registration.

As the speaker doesn't have a choice of time, he has to work to keep audience attention level high. There are many ways to add interest to the Body; choose which is appropriate for your specific occasion. The following are some suggestions:

Examples
Examples are an excellent way of keeping attention and interest, and are particularly useful to illustrate a point. When using examples ensure that:

- The example is typical and not an exceptional one.
- You use enough examples to constitute a fair sample.

Statistics
These can also be useful but make sure they are meaningful.

- Use only a few statistics at a time. Break the monotony of listing statistics by using an anecdote or visual.
- Statistics are most effectively presented by using visuals. To dramatise figures, use pictures and symbols instead of words.

Support material can make the simplest, most ordinary talk interesting. Speakers who produce interesting support material to clarify and prove their main ideas sound more authoritative and lively.

Newspapers and books are useful resources for this purpose. Books such as the *Guinness Book of Records* provide information on all subjects, such as amazing facts and statistics.

- Throughout the Body of the talk try and involve the audience. Ask for responses, or ask a rhetorical question for a change of emphasis. For example: 'How many people here today feel that safety is a major factor?' Or the rhetorical question where the speaker poses a question and then answers it himself: 'You may be wondering why we have decided to change the entry requirements . . . The reason is . . .'
- If the occasion is not serious, then humour is often appreciated by the audience, as long as it follows the general rules (see humour section). If you are using slides you could include some humorous captions or illustrations.

Again, when you have covered all your information in this section, link into the summary. You could simply say: 'And finally . . .', or 'To summarise . . .'.

THE SUMMARY

A speech is like a love affair – any fool can start one but to end one takes considerable skill.

Lord Mancroft

This is the final rounding up of your speech. It should be just that – a short, punchy ending.

- Recap your main (key) points.
- Tell the audience what action to take. For example: think about your suggestions, complete the questionnaire, support your proposal.
- Try to end on a 'high', or positive note.

PREPARING A SPEECH: INSTRUCTIONS IN DETAIL

- Thank your audience – perhaps compliment them but be sincere.
- If possible stay around for a while after you have delivered the speech. This will give the audience an opportunity to speak to you on a one-to-one basis. In any event, always let your audience know where you can be contacted; especially important if it is a business speech. Give them a business card.

When preparing a speech, many speakers work backwards on their script, i.e. they start with the conclusion. This is sound advice and I was cheered recently to hear an interview with Michael Dodds, the author. When asked how he set about writing his blockbuster thrillers, he replied that he first thought of a terrific ending, and only when he had that did he start writing the rest of the novel.

Finally, to sum it up – Sir William Harcourt believed that to produce a good speech, you should:

Think of your first sentence, then your last – and bring them as close together as possible.

Drafting and Scripting

GENERAL ADVICE

In the brainstorming session, you will have identified several areas to be covered and the key message you wish to get across to the audience. Most speakers write out their speech in full, and then revise it, taking into account the audience and the time available.

Speakers are often unsure when they should use a full script, or when brief notes or cards are more appropriate.

These guidelines, based on experience may help you decide.

FULL SCRIPT
A full script is advisable when:

- The occasion is formal.
- The speech will be recorded.
- The material is complex.
- The sequence of audio-visual aids requires fixed cues for the technical assistant.
- The speaker is inexperienced.

BRIEF NOTES
Brief notes are recommended when:

- The occasion is not too formal.
- The speech will not be recorded.
- The material does not demand a full script.
- The speaker is relatively experienced.

CARDS
Short headings are adequate when:

- The occasion is formal.

- The presentation will not be recorded.
- The material is relatively simple.
- The speaker is very experienced.

Your notes are an aid, not a hindrance. Make them brief, uncluttered and use language that is simple to understand. The next stage is actually to read the speech out loud from your notes.

When reading your presentation out loud you will have noticed points, words and phrases that need emphasis and points where you need to pause. You may also find words/ phrases which read well, but don't sound right when spoken. Use this information to develop your script; for example, underline words that you need to emphasise with a red pen and mark the pauses on your script.

Punctuation is critical and it's easier to use short sentences. However, it will sound boring if all the sentences are short, so vary their length without sacrificing the meaning.

When you have completed your script, staple the sheets together or use the card ring (punch a hole in the left hand corner of each card and hold together with a treasury tag). This method will enable you to turn over each card smoothly as you cover the information. It is also useful in the event that you drop them.

Then rehearse, rehearse.

TEXT LAYOUT

The following are some recommendations:

USE LARGE TYPE

A word processor can help you to achieve the type style you require. Major typewriter manufacturers also have a variety of type size and style options. Normal print style using upper and lower case 'letter' size can be enlarged using the 'blow-up' technique. Many printers offer this service.

DRAFTING AND SCRIPTING

LIMIT THE NUMBER OF WORDS PER LINE
Try not to have more than eight or nine words on a line. This will enable you comfortably to 'photograph' mentally roughly a line at a time.

AVOID BREAKING WORDS
Keep words intact. It is far better to carry the whole word to the next line, leaving extra space, than to break the word with a hyphen. Even compound words with hyphens should be kept on one line.

USE WIDE MARGINS
Side margins should be at least one inch on each side. Top and bottom margins should be closer to an inch and a half. This will give you lots of 'white space' around your script, making it stand out.

LINE SPACING
Leave at least double space each line. This will vary with the type style. For example, if you are using all capital letters, triple-spacing would be better.

SENTENCE SPACING
Make sure that between each full point and the start of a new sentence you have a good separation so that there is a clear break. Normally this will be two or three spaces. Again this will vary with type style.

PARAGRAPH SPACING
This will also vary with type style. As a general rule, spacing between paragraphs should be wider than your line spacing. It is also useful to indent each paragraph. This will increase the amount of 'white space' on the page, making it easier for you to keep your place and take your time.

END EACH PAGE WITH A FULL POINT
Never carry a sentence from the bottom of one page to the top of the next. Doing so causes needless delivery problems.

DRAFTING AND SCRIPTING

START EACH PAGE WITH A NEW PARAGRAPH
As no sentences are carried over from page to page, every page starts with a new sentence, which should be indented as a new paragraph. This will give you a sense of timing for a smooth page transition, as well as additional 'white space'.

AVOID LONG SENTENCES AND PARAGRAPHS
Long sentences should be shortened to two, or even three, shorter sentences. Long paragraphs should be split into shorter, more easily handled paragraphs. This will reduce the chances of losing your place.

ONE SENTENCE PARAGRAPHS
Making a key sentence a separate paragraph helps you give it the emphasis it deserves.

MARKING YOUR SCRIPT

Suspension points (...) can be used in many places instead of commas. This will improve the layout physically by providing more 'white space' which will give you a better sense of timing. Underlining key words and phrases can also help you visually. Avoid using slashes (/) to indicate pauses, which may produce a mechanical or unnatural delivery.

VISUAL AIDS AND CUES

You should clearly indicate on your script when a visual aid should be displayed and when it should be removed. This is best done in capital letters, underlined and should be placed in the middle of the page . . . not to the side.

For example:

SLIDE ON

As far as spacing is concerned, the cue instruction should be treated as a paragraph:

SLIDE OFF

Page Numbers
Page numbers can either be centred at the top of the page or placed in one of the two top corners.

Bifocal Lenses
For those with bifocal lenses, it might be easier to limit the printed information to the upper half or two-thirds of the page.

Reading Someone Else's Speech Effectively
As well as giving speeches from your own notes, there may be situations where you have to read key words inherited from others. For example:

- A speaker has been taken ill, and asks you to give his after-dinner speech.
- You must read accurate and precise instructions or statistics, e.g. presenting company accounts, sales figures.
- Reading from scripts may be the protocol of the host company/organisation.

Many Members of Parliament and Royalty have their speeches written for them. The Princess of Wales is one excellent example of how reading from a speech can work effectively. The Princess obviously rehearses her speech thoroughly. She personalises it and familiarises herself with the content, thus enabling her to put feeling into her words and phrases. She also maintains good eye contact with her audience.

You may be coerced into reading someone else's script. This can happen to the most prestigious speakers. The State Opening of Parliament in 1993 provided such an occasion.

The Queen and Prince Philip were in attendance, and all was going well until the Queen stood up to speak. To her dismay she found that she had forgotten her spectacles. With style and aplomb, she turned to the Prince, and then to the large gathering: 'My husband will give my speech.'

To have someone else deliver one's speech is the dream of most public speakers, but few have the opportunity to carry it through. On this occasion it was most successful.

Reading from scripts does not make for the most interesting speeches. However, you as the speaker should never be boring. The following are a few pointers to help you make a speech that is read as lively and interesting as one given from notes.

Familiarise Yourself with the Material

- Read through the material thoroughly. Check all pronunciations of difficult words or names. Once you have decided on the correct one, stick to this throughout.
- Divide the whole script into logical parts, and look at the content. Study the words being used, and also the feelings, emotions and attitudes beneath them.
- Indicate on your script where you will pause, or where you will add gestures. Personalise your speech. Look for places where you can insert a personal example or anecdote.
- Try to use personal pronouns. For example use 'you' when addressing the audience directly.
- Mark the script as discussed. Remember that to gain emphasis you can:
  - Change your pitch, intonation and inflection.
  - Add force or volume.
  - Vary your pace.
  - Alter your rhythm.
  - Vary your attitude.

Look at your audience and have a conversation with them. Even a written speech should sound caring and warm when read. Connect with your audience through your body language, gestures and eye contact. Check that your language is conversational in style. For example, use short forms: 'it's' instead of 'it is'.

DRAFTING AND SCRIPTING

Hints to Help your Reading Style

- Use fairly heavy paper.
- Check that the lectern is wide enough to slide the notes across with ease.
- Use only one side of the page.
- Use large bold print and have it enlarged.
- Double or triple space.
- Mark the script with all your personal instructions, pauses, etc.

Easier Script Reading
Familiarise . . . Personalise . . . Empathise . . . Practise.

Using Notes
Some people prefer to edit their full script into more manage-able proportions, usually ending up with a few sheets of A4 paper. Avoid having too many sheets, or scraps of paper, which looks untidy. If you are nervous also avoid holding a single sheet in your hand; this will certainly highlight shaking body parts.

If there are only a few sheets of paper, place a firm card behind them. The backing card at the back of an A4 pad is useful for this. This is particularly important if you intend to hold the notes.

Many people prefer to use a lectern or place their notes on a table in front of them. One of the disadvantages of using a lectern is that the speaker cannot move far from his notes. It does, however, suit the formal after-dinner speech, or a lecture. If using a lectern, number each sheet at the top left-hand corner. Display two sheets at once, and practise the smooth sliding over of the next sheet. This reduces the rustling effect which often accompanies handling notes at the lectern.

Leave sufficient space between ideas so that you can read the information easily.

The following are some general hints which you can use with either full script, notes or cards:

- Draw a margin down one side of the page or card and use this to illustrate where, for instance, you will show an overhead slide, give an example, ask a question.
- Use a red pen to underline key words. Make additional red check marks next to ideas that need emphasis.
- Underline the opening phrase in each paragraph with a highlighter pen.
- Having visual aids is another means of using notes: slides and charts can serve as an outline and information source for you.
- You can pencil notes on your overhead slide frames or even on a flipchart without your audience knowing it. A flipchart is a useful aid when speaking to small groups in an interactive situation.

Postcard-sized Cards

- Use one side only.
- Write each theme/idea on a separate card.
- When you have covered the information on the card, turn it over.
- Number each card and leave them loose. Alternatively, use a binder clip or treasury tag in one corner. You can then slip your thumb through this. (This helps keep the cards in order.)
- Index cards are ideal for this purpose. The 4 × 6 cards can be held easily in your hand like a pack of cards, with the outline typed vertically.

It does take time to prepare cards properly, but the benefits of using them far outweigh the disadvantages. They are neat and can be handled discreetly; they are also flexible. For instance, if you find yourself running out of time you can skip one or two cards (or briefly summarise each in a sentence).

You can also hold them in your hand if you need to walk about. An added bonus is that holding cards gives your hand(s) something purposeful to do, and decreases the chances of fidgeting and other negative movements.

DRAFTING AND SCRIPTING

THE TELEPROMPTER (AUTOCUE)

The teleprompter or Autocue (which is a brand name) has become more popular during the last few years. It is used by business speakers, TV presenters and also by the front bench in the House of Commons.

The teleprompter consists of a one-way screen which is placed in front of you and on to which your script is projected. The advantage of this method is that the audience can see your face through the screen, and as you read the words, you appear to be looking at the audience. The whole script is prepared in advance. The speaker needs a lot of practice, ideally with video, to be able to read the script whilst looking up at the audience for quite long periods. The full script of what you are going to say reduces nerves to manageable proportions.

The text is printed on a roll of paper or computer stationery and relayed by closed circuit television cameras through monitors near to the speaking point. From the monitor it's reflected on to the screen in front of you. An operator, hidden from the audience, carefully follows the speed at which you are speaking and moves on the roll of script as appropriate.

The advantage of using this equipment is that you can read the entire script and also maintain eye contact with the audience.

Print is normally large, with only a few words per line, therefore it is readily legible. A small table-top unit is available, which is suitable for boardroom meetings and can be used by anyone who is speaking.

Hints for Using the Autocue

- Preparation is the key to success. Allow yourself sufficient time for last-minute changes. Send your script to the teleprompt company in plenty of time. This is particularly important if several speakers are involved. When modifications are made at the last minute, all the cues must be re-positioned.
- Always ask for a copy of the script typed on the Autocue roll,

- so that you can practise reading aloud.
- Allow several run-throughs with the teleprompt company at the venue. It is the normal procedure for the teleprompt hire company to include some tuition in their hire charge.
- Check the height of the screen, as this can be adjusted to suit different speakers. If you place the screen vertically, this allows for a greater range of speaker's height, without adjustment.
- Consider the use of two or more screens. It gives the reader more flexibility of movement, but remember this will need extra practice.
- Appear natural, look away from the screen now and again.
- Speak at a normal pace.

Whether you use a full script or notes depends on the formality of the occasion, and the experience of the speaker. When well managed, both can be effective. The following observations may help you decide which will suit you best.

Keeping Audience Interest: General Advice

QUOTATIONS

I often quote myself. It adds spice to my conversation.
George Bernard Shaw

Your audience has come to hear you speak. But that is no reason why you cannot use the thoughts of others. Quoting other people is an art in itself. Here are two suggestions on how best to perfect it.

- Reading long quotations at length or from memory is no substitute for using your own words and thoughts. Choose short quotations which are relevant to your speech. Attribute your chosen quotation to its true author, if you can. If in doubt, you could try: 'Was it Oscar Wilde who said . . .?' or 'I think it was Shakespeare who once remarked that . . .'
- If the attribution is to someone in your own lifetime, you could try: 'I once heard Margaret Thatcher . . .' No one can disprove this.

For more advice on how to use quotations, see the chapter **Useful Quips and Quotations**, page 194.

VISUAL AIDS

Most speeches can be delivered without the use of visual aids. However, there is a certain type of speech usually called a

32

'presentation' where the use of visuals can enhance speaker performance. Situations where the use of visual aids is advised, and often necessary, mostly fall into the 'business' category: for example, presenting ideas or information to business clients.

Increasingly, more and more informal clubs and organisations invite guest speakers to talk about their particular area of expertise. For example I am often asked to talk to management groups about speaking in public. These occasions often take the form of a seminar and can last up to a couple of hours. The type of visual aids I use will be determined by the venue and the number of people attending. The following examples will help illustrate this:

Example One

Brief: To speak to a group of women in management about speaking in public.

Objective: To give advice and hints on the above, and to answer any questions they may have about the subject.

Time: One hour (forty-five minutes talk followed by fifteen minutes questions).

Audience: Between twenty and forty managers interested to learn more about the subject.

In this case my brief was quite clear. I knew my objective, who would be in the audience, and how long the speech should last. These are always the minimum requirements before you should take into consideration which visual aids to use. The host organisation offered to provide a flipchart and also an overhead projector, which I used on this occasion.

When considering whether to use visuals ask two questions:

● Is it appropriate for this audience and subject, i.e. will everybody in the audience be able to see clearly?

33

KEEPING AUDIENCE INTEREST: GENERAL ADVICE

- Will the use of visuals enhance my performance, i.e. add to audience appreciation/interest/understanding of the subject?

As a general rule of thumb, overhead slides provide:

SPEAKER CONTROL
Not only can the audience see the slides, but so can you. This offers you better control of the group and more eye contact. You will be more receptive to their reactions.

IDENTIFICATION
Overhead slides illustrate what you are saying. They are also flexible, as you can turn off the projector to elaborate or make a point, or build up information as you progress through the speech.

FACILITATION
The overhead projector is easy to use, particularly the most up-to-date models which offer little distraction.

Overhead slides work best with smaller audiences. Always check that the people at the back of the room can see them clearly.

Use 35mm slides with large audiences, and where you need to reproduce images of photographic quality.

I made use of the flipchart for the interactive session after my talk, for example to illustrate a point, draw a diagram, or when responding to questions.

Flipcharts are excellent aids, particularly useful for group discussion and brainstorming activities. They are best used with groups of up to about thirty people. Many people feel that flipcharts are not cost effective, and therefore avoid using them.

If you decide that the flipchart would provide a useful aid for your purpose, then there are a variety of types on the market. One consists of laminated boards (available in different colour combinations) which can be wiped and re-used. There is a chart on the market which also acts as a photocopier. What is written on the chart can be duplicated. This would be particularly useful for group and committee meetings, where everyone could have an instant copy of discussions. The quality of the input to the chart will, of course, determine the quality of output, but there may be occasions where it would be beneficial to take away a hard copy rather than make notes. This highlights the main fear people have about using a flipchart, i.e. that their writing is illegible. There is more advice on how to overcome this under **Hints on Visual Aids** at the end of this section.

Example Two

Brief: To give a talk to members of the local Chamber of Commerce.

Objective: To talk about the use of quotations in speeches, and answer any general questions they may have.

Time: Thirty minutes followed by questions.

Audience: Twenty-five members of the Chamber.

Instead of using an overhead projector, I decided to use my Quotation books as props. I set up the books on the table in front of me, where they could be seen, and then picked the appropriate book up as I talked about it. After question time, the audience had the opportunity to handle and look through the books at their leisure.

Hints on Visual Aids

35MM SLIDES
These are less flexible than overhead slides. Their main advantage is that they can effectively dramatise a difficult concept. Their chief disadvantage is that they turn the audience's attention away from you, and also require a

35

darkened room to be viewed effectively.

Your voice has to be especially lively and interesting if your presentation takes place in darkness, particularly if the slides are shown after a meal. Despite their obvious disadvantages, in many cases slides can be invaluable for larger audiences. Some situations really call for their use, for example, to present in an instant what would take many words to convey. Slides also give the speaker flexibility; individual slides can be replaced or updated fairly easily without changing the whole set.

To produce effective slides:

- Build your slides around what you want your audience to remember (your objectives).
- Establish a good rapport with your audience before you begin the slide show. To do this, face the audience and:
  - deliver your introduction (remember, tell them what you are going to tell them)
  - dim lights and link into your slides (main body)
  - with lights on . . . link into your summary and close.

If you use this sequence, you begin and end your talk with audience eye contact.

- Don't leave a slide on the screen longer than you have to. When you have finished talking about it, go on to the next one.
- Prepare the technical aspects well. Check that:
  - the projector is in good condition
  - the projector is in focus
  - the slides are placed in the carousel the right way round.
    To do this:
  - hold the slide to the projector light so that you can read it.
  - place the slide in the carousel upside down, so that the top of the slide enters first
  - number each slide
  - check the slides are in order and practise with the remote control
  - use only as many slides as you really need. Don't waste

the audience's attention with superfluous information.

If something goes wrong with the slides – if you drop the carousel, or they are out of order, or the lights fail, or there is some other emergency – take a break and try to fix it.

The speaker is the best person to operate the projector.

Stand where you feel comfortable and where you are not blocking the screen. Remote control enables you to stand well away from the projector, perhaps at the side of the room. If someone else is operating the slide projector, then rehearse together – you must have confidence in the projectionist. Work out any codes to exchange information. Cueing can best be done by marking the script with cue key words.

OVERHEAD SLIDES

Producing overhead slides (often referred to as OHPs) is relatively easy and cheap. Copy bureaux can design and pre-pare them very quickly. Most companies now have graphics terminals and plotters available in-house. If you have a pre-pared speech which you will be asked to deliver on several occasions, then it is well worth having a set of overheads made up. Providing you don't need to change any of the information contained in them, they will last for years.

Some hints on overhead slide technique:

- For a professional talk, always have your overheads pre-pared professionally. Avoid the temptation of writing on them, as this is usually messy. The exception is in an informal group discussion where the OHP may be used as you would the flipchart.
- Place your first overhead on the projector before switching on.
- Turn the projector on and off, depending on whether you want the spotlight on yourself or to share it with a slide.
- Place a pointer (pen or pencil will do) on the portion of your slide to which you want to draw attention.

- Be selective: a few good visuals are often better than many. Too many visuals may dilute the key points. The number of visuals may depend on how graphic your information is and to some degree on how long you plan to talk. There have been effective talks with just one visual.

Transparencies of printed information from books and magazines will usually not be large enough to be legible when they are projected, so be careful to select material which has printing at least as large as Orator 10 font.

FLIPCHARTS

This visual aid is useful but limited to small groups. One of the commonest complaints from the audience when this equipment is in use relates to their inability to actually see what has been written; usually because the speaker is standing in front of it.

To avoid this, stand to one side of the chart stand, on the right if you are right-handed and on the left if you are left-handed. To check correct positioning, try this. Grasp the edge of the chart with your left hand and move it slightly back to your right. Your arm should now be fully extended. Think of your gripping arm as a hinge. This means that you will cover part of the board as you write. By swinging back on the 'hinge', you can reveal what you have written to the people on your right.

If you are apprehensive about using the flipchart – perhaps you feel that your handwriting is not good enough to be seen, or you can't write in a straight line – then choose one of the many types of chart available with lined or graphed paper. Another way of getting round this is to prepare your chart in advance, so that you only have to turn over the pages as you cover your points.

The pencil technique is also useful if you want to reduce time spent working on the chart. To do this, lightly sketch out your graph, diagram, or figures in pencil. At the appropriate time in your speech you can then quickly go over your work using a coloured pen. I have seen this used very successfully on numerous occasions by speakers. It is particularly impressive if the speaker uses different coloured pens. (This method of pre-preparing the flipchart also reduces the time the speaker spends with his back to the audience.)

General guidelines when using the flipchart:

- Don't talk and write at the same time.
- Use key words instead of sentences so that you cut down the writing time.
- Stand back to allow the audience to read it.
- Write in large clear lettering.

Summary
The more of the audience's senses you use, the more effectively you communicate. Visuals also increase your listeners' retention; verbalised messages can easily be either misinterpreted or forgotten, but visual aids used correctly can help increase retention.

For visual aids to benefit you, they must be effectively prepared and handled. Make sure that they clarify information rather than confusing it.

Checklist for Good Visual Aids

- Good visuals are: legible, appropriate, up-to-date, well designed, accurate, realistic, manageable, meaningful and necessary.
- Keep the information on your slides simple. Keep information to a minimum.
- Use colour to add impact and interest.
- Always put a title at the top of each slide.
- Use a different colour to make this stand out.
- Both vertical and horizontal (often referred to as portrait and landscape) formats work well. This is a matter of choice. Perhaps use both for variety.
- Before presenting visuals, brief your audience on the material each will cover.
- Explain the key points during the talk.
- Handle them smoothly.

- Present them in their most effective sequence.
- Make sure that everyone can see them clearly, and that neither you nor the equipment is in the way.

USING HUMOUR

People enjoy laughing. Humour relaxes your audience and often acts as a good ice-breaker, but don't use humour just for the sake of it. Make sure that the subject matter is appropriate to your audience and your situation. Here are some tips for using humour in speeches:

- Always consider the feelings of your audience. Make sure your jokes are in good taste, i.e. nothing sexist, racist, ageist. If there is any possibility that you might give offence, even to one person in the audience, leave it out.
- The safest joke is about yourself; this will always guarantee a laugh.
- An original joke works best, because your audience will not have heard it before.
- Laugh with and not at the person whom you make the butt of your joke.
- The punch line of a joke relies on surprise.

What if No One Laughs?
This is one of the common fears when using humour. If a joke goes down like a lead balloon, both the speaker and the audience will feel embarrassed. Good speakers are aware of audience reaction, and will be watching for signs of approval. If you can tell that a joke has not gone down well, by the look of disapproval on the faces of your audience, then quickly change tack. Accept the fact that you have misjudged either your material or the audience. If for instance you are delivering the Best Man's speech and you realise there is a problem, then concentrate on getting the audience back on your side. Say pleasant things about the bride and groom and pass on your warmest wishes for their future happiness.

Body Language

The body never lies
                    Martha Graham

GENERAL ADVICE

The loudest statement a speaker makes is emitted before he opens his mouth: he tells the audience with a whole series of signals how he feels. If the message conveyed is nervous and non-assertive, then everything that follows is transmitted on that frequency, and consequently fails to make an impact.

You should consciously use body language when you are making a speech.

USE IT TO:

- Invite a response or a contribution.
- Develop empathy and build trusting relationships.
- Present yourself effectively – develop your image and self-confidence. Remember, first impressions last.
- Give feedback (e.g. I am listening, interested, concerned, enthusiastic).
- Set the scene so as to relax the audience.
- Show the audience that you are happy to be talking to them.

When considering body language, always stay within the limits of comfort. Uncalled-for displays of body language create unnecessary risk.

Research shows that the totality of the message you project comprises:

55% appearance and body language

41

38% how you sound
7% what you say

A combination of all three elements creates a very powerful message and the signals received by the audience will say, 'This speaker is confident, competent and in control.'

The personal body language or non-verbal element of your communication must be positive to make a good impression. The components of the message you send can be divided into these three groups.

Voice

- pace of speech
- clarity
- pitch
- volume
- tone
- expressiveness

Your Body

- appearance
- facial expression
- eye contact
- posture
- the way you move
- the gestures you make

Relationship to Others

USE OF TOUCH, SENSITIVITY TO AND USE OF PERSONAL SPACE
You must use body language consciously and deliberately. Research has shown that when the verbal and non-verbal messages are in conflict, the audience will believe the non-verbal message. An actor manages to produce laughter when he combines one non-verbal gesture with a verbal statement

to the opposite effect. The disparity between verbal and non-verbal is always enough to make the audience laugh.

Of all body language, it is bearing that communicates presence the most quickly and effectively. Bad posture, sloppy sitting, slumped standing, weary walking are common faults. The message sent out here is interpreted as 'Who cares?' Remember no matter what the speaking engagement, the message you want to relay is confidence, competence and control. Here is some advice to help you do this.

POSTURE

The key to holding yourself well is the simple but contrasting phrase 'relaxed authority'. A batsman or a golfer, before he shapes to hit the ball, stands with relaxed alertness.

Stand easy and upright, the stomach in, the chest well held, the head well poised and the feet comfortably apart. Keep the feet still. Then, as you speak, turn smoothly from left to right, using all the joints given you for this purpose – the ankles, the knees, the hips and the shoulders. Particularly give the head the fuller mobility it commands through the top two bones of the vertebral column, allowing it to move sideways, upwards, downwards, forwards and backwards. This is a natural action, and will help you as a speaker. This gives the nervous tension and nervous energy a healthy outlet.

Tension that might have been shown in fidgeting, excessive feet movements or gesturing, is used up unnoticeably. Learn to stand tall with your head and chin up, your ribcage high, your stomach tucked in. When you are standing, push your head up as high as you can – feel it stretching. Then let your shoulders slump, as if you were trying to lift a heavy object from the floor.

Keep your feet slightly apart with the weight evenly distributed. If you hold the legs close together, your movement is distinctly cramped. By all means, occasionally shift your ground – say, every five minutes – but do so unhurriedly. There must never be any unnecessary movement of any part of the body. Check that all your movements are purposeful.

If you are delivering your speech from a stage, lectern, or from behind a table, as in the after-dinner or wedding speech, there is less opportunity for movement. Certain speaking situations may justify movement, for example:

- If you are demonstrating something, you may need to move closer to your listeners so they can see better.
- If you want to write on a flipchart, or change an overhead slide.
- If you move forward into the audience to take questions.
- If you want to reinforce a change of mood. For example the speaker may stand behind a table for the first part of the speech. For the second, he may move forward to take questions or give a demonstration.

Occasionally there are circumstances where the speaker will remain seated during the speech. For example by custom of the meeting, through injury or illness, or more often, as a member of a panel, answering questions after a speech. In this case, a position of relaxed authority is not only for appearance but, as always, for good breathing and the comfort of your throat.

Be aware of your posture at all times, particularly if you are waiting to stand up and speak. Sitting back in a passive position makes you look laid back and inert. By projecting your upper body towards the speaker, you are thrusting yourself actively into the scene where the action is. Bad posture whilst sitting or standing is very tiring. Develop a good posture, it will help you reduce fatigue and exhaustion.

A little trick which will instil audience confidence in you is to face them with an open body at all times. No folded arms across the chest, or limp arms by the side.

Never turn your back on the audience. To help you remember this, think of the words 'full frontal'. (This may remind you to smile now and again.)

GESTURE

A relaxed, responsive and smooth series of movements helps the audience to relax. It will also be easier for you to listen creatively, to smile and gesture as appropriate. Erratic movements signal bad news to the audience: the message is that you are tense, nervous and worried. Such an attitude in turn evokes a negative response: uncertainty and distrust. There are two ways most people move about; smoothly and slowly, or jerkily and swiftly. Aim for the former.

EXPRESSION

It is a psychological fact that facial expressions alter emotions and that in time we grow in tune with our most usual expression. Cultivate a pleasant and positive expression. Smile occasionally and when appropriate, for example when you answer a question, or make reference to your audience. A twinkle in the eye automatically causes a twinkle in the voice. This quality is of vital importance in all speeches, particularly in the after-dinner type.

Many doctors believe that smiling produces hormones which have a positive influence on body functions. Looking happy can actually pick you up!

Think of this just before you stand up to speak, smile and tell yourself that you are going to enjoy making this speech. Imagine the applause you will receive afterwards.

HANDS

'What should I do with my hands?' This is one of the commonest challenges for the public speaker. People do many things with their hands whilst making a speech. Here are some of the most common:

- Drinking.

45

- Clutching the back of a chair.
- Fiddling with loose change in pocket.
- Playing with pointer, pen, notes.
- Grasping table or lectern.
- Wringing, rubbing.
- Shuffling cue cards.
- Adopting one of the following poses:
  - The fig leaf position; hands clasped in front of the body.
  - Duke of Edinburgh; hands clasped behind back.
  - Frustrated housewife; tidies up paper, notes on table.
  - The orchestra conductor; waves pen in the air.

Most speakers have a favourite pose, such as hands loosely held in front. The secret is to find a position which suits your style and comfort level. Never clasp your hands together, or hold a wrist tightly. Artificial control reveals tension – and can actually stiffen the expression. Whatever position you adopt, don't let your hands flit about. Properly used, movement of the hands is part of your expression of thought. Here are some ideas of what you might do with them.

- Cradle them just under the ribs – the right hand gently resting on the left palm with left thumb locking both together.
- Clasp them in front of the body.
- Hold them by your side at arm's length, the backs showing slightly (this suits a quiet speaker or a quiet passage in a speech).
- Hold cards to nestle in the palm of the hand (lift forward and up when referring to them).

Many speakers like to hold cards in the palm of their hand, a pen if writing on the flipchart, or a pointer if using over-heads. There is no hard and fast rule on this, except that whatever you decide, make sure that it is not the centre of attention. The audience are there to listen to you, not to see you shuffling your note cards, snapping the top of your pen, or pulling the pointer in and out. Try to hold only one item in your hand, preferably your cards or notes.

POSITIVE ATTITUDE

This is one of the key elements to successful speaking. On the surface, attitude is the way you communicate your mood to others. When you are optimistic and anticipate successful encounters you transmit a positive attitude. People will warm to you and respond favourably. Attitude is a mind-set. It is the way you look at things mentally – whether you see situations as either opportunities or failures, whether you view giving a speech as a chore or an opportunity.

Adopting a positive and pleasant attitude will bring you many benefits. A friendly style will help build bridges with your audience, and you will feel less nervous and more confident.

Always use positive language. Eliminate the negative. For example I have heard a speaker start a speech by saying, 'This is not a very interesting subject.'

If you use language like this, the audience will switch off, and in fact become resentful that you are taking up their time.

The benefits of delivering a speech with enthusiasm are as follows:

- Your audience will warm to you, and therefore they will be more attentive. (Audiences generally adopt the tone of the speaker: enthusiastic presenter = enthusiastic audience; dull, boring speaker = audience switch off.)
- Enthusiasm will help:
  - Your voice will sound more interesting: an enthusiastic voice breathes life, not monotony.
  - Your body language will be more positive, i.e. verbals and non-verbals will match. Natural expressions, gestures, posture will result.
  - Enthusiasm is catching – enthuse your audience.

First Impressions

DRESS

I take ruthless stock of myself in the mirror before going out. A polo jumper or unfortunate tie exposes one to great danger.

Noel Coward

The essential factors which shape your decisions about dress must be the occasion and your attitude to the people attending it. Your appearance should be appropriate to you, your position and your message. People dislike the phoney, so whatever clothes you choose to wear, make sure that you feel comfortable in them. If you are uncomfortable, this feeling of unease will transmit itself to the audience.

Clothes make a statement about you, and everything about you sends signals, the old school or club tie, the Armani suit, a woman's too revealing neckline, bad grooming, scuffed shoes. People tend to dress according to the group in which they belong. Take care that the statement is going out with the message you want to send, or is at least composed of information you wish to go out.

Occasions such as weddings and celebratory events are somewhat easier to plan for in the way of dress, as convention takes precedence. At the same time, even a smart morning suit or dinner jacket can look shabby if some general rules are not followed.

Here is a checklist of some things to avoid.

FOR MEN

- Ill-fitting suit.
- Bulging pockets (avoid coins, handkerchiefs, keys).

48

- Pens/pencils in top pocket.
- Excessive aftershave.
- Unbuttoned shirts.
- Loud ties.
- White socks.
- Light coloured shoes.
- Flashy cuff-links, tie pins, jewellery.
- Ostentatious belt buckles.
- Short socks.
- Check zips and buttons are secured.

FOR WOMEN

- Bare legs.
- Very high heels, short skirts, low cut blouses.
- Distracting jewellery, jangling bracelets, earrings.
- Large belt buckles.
- Shoes with scuffed heels.
- Lumps and lines – check what is underneath.
- Standing against bright light if wearing lightweight clothing.
- Excessive make-up, perfume.
- Distracting hairstyle, e.g. hanging over face.
- Taking your handbag to the lectern/table. (Leave it to one side.)
- Check zips and buttons are secured.

As you can see most of this advice is common sense, but it is amazing the number of speeches which I have sat through where the speaker has thrown caution to the wind. At one particular after-dinner event, the guest speaker delivered an amusing account of life in the fast lane, as managing director of an international company. He kept the audience enthralled and entertained as he talked of the 'cut and thrust' and 'life at the sharp end'. This might have been less entertaining for the audience and less embarrassing for him, if he had bothered to check his zip before standing up to speak!

On another occasion a famous actor delivered his speech with one hand in his pocket. His words rang out with enthusiasm, to the musical accompaniment of jingling coins and jangling keys.

General Hints for Both Men and Women

- A dark business suit, teamed with a smart shirt or blouse, is seen as 'professional' for both men and women.
- Take care with shoes. Scuffed heels are very noticeable on women in particular. Shoes are particularly visible if you are speaking from a raised platform.
- If you have to travel to a speaking engagement, if possible, carry your outfit in a suit carrier and change when you arrive.
- Adapt your dress to the people you are addressing; you don't want to dress exactly like them, but choose a style similar to theirs. When in doubt, dress on the formal side, but try to add some flair; audiences don't want to look at deliberately drab speakers.
- Don't wear clothes that need to be adjusted when you stand up or sit down.
- If you wear glasses, remember that heavy rims will hide your face and interfere with eye contact. Stay away from strong tinting or light-sensitive lenses that darken under lighting. Many professional speakers avoid these problems by opting for contact lenses.
- Use your glasses to effect by taking them off once or twice during your presentation. Use them to give your gestures added impact. Take them off at the end of your speech to take questions.
- Aim to be well groomed and well turned out – fresh and neat; then forget your appearance, let your personality shine through.

DEVELOPING YOUR OWN STYLE

Style is effectiveness of assertion.

George Bernard Shaw

True style comes from within, and a person with style is said to possess 'charisma'. Style and commercial success are synonymous. Body language is part of your style. If you discover that your natural style is to talk very quickly and move in jerky spasms, try to slow down the rate of speech and examine your body movements. The likelihood is that if you can control your speed, the movements will also slow down and become less jerky. Keep your own 'natural' style. If you are comfortable being voluble and moving your hands and body as you speak, tone this down only if it is excessive and causes a distraction. Don't try to change the total you, but make small changes for improvement.

I have watched presenters who have broken all the so-called rules of body language, loud excessive body movements, infringements of body space, who have performed with excellence – their own natural style of humour, friendliness and enthusiasm have turned a negative to a positive. Tom Peters, author and management guru, is such a speaker. He recently conducted a one-day seminar in London attended by six hundred business people. He kept this large gathering enthralled throughout the day as he shared with them his thoughts and theories on the future of organisations. His innovative ideas and captivating style completely over-shadowed his excessive hand and body movements as he paced the stage.

I have also witnessed speakers who try to 'adopt a style' that quite clearly is far removed from their own natural style. The result is a wooden and lacklustre performance, punctuated with incongruent body language.

Feedback is also an essential ingredient of good communication. Just as your audience will be reading your signals, you will be reading theirs!

What to Look For
Think of your audience like flowers.

- *Closed*, and they are defensive, negative.
- *Open*, and they are warm and receptive.
- *Head down*, = negative.
- *Head comes up*, = interested.

51

- *Head to the side*, perhaps with finger vertical up to the cheekbone = evaluating, deeply interested.

If you are boring, covering known ground, then the audience gets impatient, tapping, twitching, and fiddling with things. If they have had enough, they turn to something else, such as a diary or another paper. They look at their watch or the clock; they even look longingly at the door!

If they are bored, they become lethargic, stop looking at you and put their heads down on their hands, eyes half shut. People move all the time. Look for feedback, and match how you perform to how they react. Unless you must stick to a script, be driven by your audience, not your notes. If the audience turns off, you waste your time and theirs.

APPEARANCE AND BODY LANGUAGE CHECKLIST

- Dress smartly and be well groomed. Remember 'PMA' – dress should be appropriate to your **position**, your **message**, your **audience**. It should reflect your personal style.
- 'Upright' posture – head up, shoulders back, chest out, stomach in, back straight.
- Stand up – full frontal to your audience.
- Get as close to the audience as possible without invading their personal space.
- Smile occasionally – but not at individuals, unless specifically referring to them.
- Project your voice to the back of the room.
- Make gestures and movements appropriate to your individual style, but always purposeful.
- Speak with enthusiasm – bring some passion to your subject.
- Relax and enjoy yourself.

Summary
Appearance and body language are important elements to consider if you wish to create a positive and professional image.

FIRST IMPRESSIONS

Here is some advice from Sir Peter Ustinov, a man with his own unique style.

The main thing is to have a point of view, and to release your imagination in the parkland of your subject, like a dog. Then, as the dog does, rely on instinct. Don't go on too long. If the public is wonderful, stop a little short of total triumph. If they find you boring, go on a little longer than necessary, just to punish them. Also resist the temptation to laugh at your jokes before reaching the point. The audience may find this inhibiting, to the point of not wishing to join in the laughter, your laughter. There are many rules, but as usual, they are only to be broken.

Controlling Nerves

The human brain starts the moment you are born and
never stops until you stand up to speak in public.
Sir George Jessel

Anyone who has ever had to stand up and speak in public will
identify with the above. The fear of standing up and making a
fool of yourself or forgetting what you were going to say
produces all kinds of symptoms. Here are a few of the most
common.

- Shallow breathing.
- Dry mouth.
- Static posture.
- Hand, leg and knee shake.
- Rapid speech.
- Sweaty palms.
- Palpitations and feelings of panic.
- Blotchiness on face and neck.
- Nausea.
- Negative body language, e.g. poor eye contact.

Most speakers have experienced some if not all of these
symptoms when asked to speak in public. It is a positive sign to
feel apprehensive about making a speech. Many experienced
speakers talk of being nervous before a 'performance', but they
have learned to harness their adrenalin flow to their advantage.
With thorough preparation, a little nervousness is a good sign.
It means that you realise the importance of the occasion and
want to do your best. Sometimes anxiety can block the enjoyment of the occasion, but there are some simple steps you can
adopt to help.

CONTROLLING NERVES

Keep Breathing

This is one of the simplest exercises which can be done anywhere. Try it in the period before you give your speech.

- Draw in a good deep breath.
- Release air slowly, counting to ten out loud.
- Continue until you build up a rhythm.

Another useful exercise is The Flop.

- Exhale, bending over your stomach.
- Now stand straight and slowly breathe in deeply through your mouth.
- Repeat twice.

This exercise should make you feel relaxed and energised. Be careful not to overdo it, because too much oxygen may make you dizzy.

Energy Generator

- Sit in a straight-back chair. Carry your ribcage high, but not in a ramrod-straight military position. Incline slightly forward.
- Now put your hands together just in front of your chest, your elbows akimbo, your fingertips pointing upward, and push so that you feel an isometric opposing force in the heels of your palms and under your arms.
- Say 'ssss', like a hiss. As you're exhaling the sound, contract the muscles in the vital triangle as though you were rowing a boat against a current, pulling the oars back. The vital triangle should feel like a tightening corset.
- Relax the muscles at the end of your exhalation, then inhale gently.

Contracting those muscles prevents the production of noradrenaline and epinephrine, the fear-producing chemicals in your system. So, when you want to shake off nervousness, sit with your vital triangle contracted, your lips slightly parted and release your breath over your lower teeth on a silent hiss.

You can do this anywhere.

When you feel nervous, keep in mind that:

- Fear is a normal experience. The fact that you are afraid indicates that you are like most other people.
- Fears are not well founded: speakers do not die while speaking, or even faint. Audiences usually receive them sympathetically.
- Unless you are presenting a thesis to which the audience seriously objects, your audience will want you to succeed.
- Speakers who are well prepared almost always give creditable performances.
- Nervousness tends to disappear with added experience.
- Speakers seldom look as frightened as they feel. Audiences rarely see a speaker's knees tremble, or face flush.
- The tension you feel at the beginning of the talk is helpful. Speakers who no longer find an audience stimulating are likely to be dull. Use the nervous energy to sharpen your delivery and concentrate on getting your points across.

In conclusion, follow these guidelines to help you overcome your fear:

- Tell a story from your personal experience. Your audience is interested in you. For many, the most relaxing way to begin any presentation is to explain how you came to be involved with your topic.
- Think about relaxing your audience. Put your audience at ease.
- Think positive: concentrate on being yourself, rather than thinking about how nervous you feel. Change your tension into enthusiasm for your subject. Visualise yourself making a successful speech.

CONTROLLING NERVES

Pitfalls for the Nervous

The quickest route to fluency is Macon Blanc.

It is very difficult for speakers to resist the temptation to have a drink before delivering their speech. Particularly on the after-dinner and celebratory occasions, where good food and wine are part of the enjoyment of the celebration. Beware! Dutch courage can do more harm than good.

If your throat is dry, stick to mineral water. Sip water during pauses in your speech. If you sip alcohol while you speak, you will give the impression of being desperate. If you feel it will help, try to stick to one drink before you rise. One drink may stimulate and relax you; any more, and your thought processes will slow down, speech may become slurred and your reflexes will be clumsy. Try to eat a minimum of food, however delicious. Too much food could also slow you down, or perhaps give you indigestion.

If you are delivering your speech from behind a table or lectern, common for business speeches, you may find a jug of water placed before you on the table top. Before you start your speech, remove the water (or coffee etc.), and place it away from the table. I have witnessed many speeches which have literally been a washout. It is difficult to recover credibility if you accidentally spill liquid over your notes or overheads.

Finally, when applause greets your final words and you sit down, you will experience a rush of adrenalin. You have acquitted yourself well, and are relieved it's all over. Watch out for signs of over excitability. That knotted stomach may have prevented you from eating earlier, but now you want to eat and drink everything in sight. Remember you want to live to perform again!

Timing and Editing

TIMING

The point of satiation is reached very soon after the peak
of popularity.

Dr Johnson

It is essential that you know the time allocated for your speech.
On more formal occasions you may be asked to speak for
upwards of fifteen minutes, and many can last for up to an hour.

Timing for wedding speeches is normally left to the discretion
of the speakers, but ten to fifteen minutes is a reasonable
speaking time for the principal speakers.

Speakers often find that timing is one of the most difficult
areas to gauge accurately. Don't worry about your timing until
you have edited your material and have at least a first draft of
your notes. Mark time checks on each card (or page). One key
point per card will help you do this.

Allocate the elapsed time from the start to the climax of each
key point. Do not use actual times, as start time for speeches
can run early or late. Mark these times on your notes, say every
three minutes for a short speech, or five for a longer one. As
you progress through the speech you can slow down, speed up,
cut; introduce extra items as necessary in order to finish at the
exact time. Rehearse your speech until your timing is right.

Many speakers find it useful to place their watch on the table
in front of them.

EDITING

When you have drafted your speech, do a few dry runs. This

will help you get the feel of the words and phrases. Be ruthless when you edit your script. Take out parts which hold up the flow, such as long-winded explanations or anecdotes. Also delete material which is not relevant to your topic.

When advising on editing material, I always ask new presenters to remind themselves of the objectives of the speech. For example, imagine you are a sports personality asked to give an after-dinner speech about becoming an Olympic gold medallist. Clearly this is a very broad subject, and an enthusiastic speaker could probably talk for many hours on this subject.

If you are given a broad topic such as this, try and condense it into something more manageable. Start by giving the speech a title – *Steps to Success*. Your objectives would then be to outline how you achieved this. The subject is then easily divided in three or four areas (this is a good number for any type and length of speech).

For example:

Title: *Steps to Success*
- how I became interested in sport
- career history
- Olympic Games.

This provides a good *structure* for the speech. Once you have included a few interesting points and anecdotes in each section and rehearsed, then you can do a final edit. To do this:

Think about how much time you have to speak. For example if your total speech is forty minutes, you may decide to spend five minutes introducing the topic, then ten minutes in each section, leaving five minutes to summarise.

Now, go through your script and look at the content. Ask yourself of each point – is this relevant to the subject and audience, do they need to know this information or can I leave it out? This is often called the MUST rule – retaining essential information to encourage audience understanding and enjoyment. This method will help you identify important points which should be included. You could then look at these and see if you could perhaps tell them with more humour or feeling.

Delivery

My dear mother-in-law only projects her voice when
calling for a gin.

Michael Aspel

YOUR VOICE

Many people worry about how they speak and how they sound.
Often this anxiety prevents them from expressing themselves as
fully as they would wish. We spend 80% of our time speaking
and listening, and yet these are often the areas which are
neglected.

Much research has gone into how we communicate. A recent
communications survey found that of a number of frequently
encountered speaking habits, the following were found to be
the most annoying to the audience.

- Mumbling or talking too softly.
- Monotonous boring voice.
- Using filler words such as 'um' and 'you know'.
- Talking too fast.
- Using poor grammar or mispronouncing words.

Your audience will be judging you partly by how you talk. They
are making decisions about you, which may or may not be
accurate, and they will act on these perceptions. The first step
to improvement is to look at and listen to yourself. Objectively
see and hear yourself the way others perceive you. A video-
camera and recorder are excellent tools to help you assess your
performance, and also to monitor improvements. A tape
recorder is needed to help you analyse your voice.

DELIVERY

If you don't have a video recorder, then stand in front of a mirror and use a tape recorder.

Many people are surprised, and often horrified, when they hear themselves for the first time. Their voice does not sound in the least as they had imagined. It seems to sound higher in pitch and thinner in quality. Often there are mannerisms which are totally unexpected – you speak slower or faster than you think, you sound affected, or sloppy with unfinished consonants, or your accent may be heavier than you thought. Worst of all you may sound plain, flat and boring.

Remember that there are many other impressions, such as communication through the eyes, face and body, all of which influence how we hear a person and tell us something. It is interesting what images we create of speakers on the radio (and the telephone), based purely on voice. It is often a shock, pleasant or unpleasant, to see the actual person – the voice and body seem mismatched.

If you are rehearsing at home, look in the mirror to see how you are making the sounds. Observe your body language, i.e. your facial expression and stance. At this stage you are primarily concerned with your voice, but it is worth noting down any observations at this stage, then reading the section on body language.

Whatever method you use for rehearsal – tape recorder, video, mirror, or a friend to give you feedback – answer the following questions. This will give you a checklist for improvement.

COMMUNICATION CHECKLIST

Does your voice sound:

	Yes	No
Shrill or squeaky		
Too loud		
Too high		
Monotonous		

DELIVERY

Pronunciation
Do you:

	Yes	No
Mumble		
Mispronounce words		
Have an accent or dialect		
Mispronounce vowels		

General communication skills
Do you:

	Yes	No
Talk too fast		
Talk too slowly		
Tail off at the end of sentences		
Use clichés, slang, jargon		
Say 'um' or 'okay' or use fillers		

Other comments:
e.g. body language

Listen to your tape or video objectively. Imagine that you are criticising someone other than yourself. It is even more valuable if you can persuade a friend to help you do this. This checklist will help you identify areas of your vocal image which need improvement.

VERBAL COMMUNICATION

Clear Diction
There is no excuse for sloppy speech. Naturally you are influenced by the particular regional accent of your birth, your parents and the general community. Everyone has an accent, and if you can put your message across so that you are understood by those who are listening to you, then your accent is an asset, and can only count in your favour. Be aware of your

posture: head up and look at your audience. Speak clearly and distinctly.

Modulation

The enemy of modulation is monotony – speaking in a one-note drone. Most people are not guilty of monotony, but are guilty of dull and lifeless speaking. Modulation of the voice depends on momentary changes of pace, of pitch and of power; and on pausing. Grasp this comforting point from the beginning, the mastery of these attributes not only allows you to appear more accomplished to the audience, but also allows you to speak more easily. To speak monotonously, or just without colour or tone, is not only disagreeable to those listening but more fatiguing for you, because you are using only one set of muscles.

Projection

People normally lack resonance of voice because they do not make full use of the lungs and the many resonant cavities of the head and upper body; because the jaw muscles have become rigid, the mouth has become tight and the tongue physically lazy.

Exercise

Humming is a useful exercise to help projection. Hum on the letter 'M', which means that the lips to all intents and purposes are closed and you are using the post-nasal cavities.

The word to have burnt into your brain all the time you are humming is 'forward!' Speaking from the front of the mouth is essential for good audibility; for the ability to carry your words to the furthest point that your eyes must look. The proof that you are humming correctly is that very soon the inside of your lips, particularly of the upper lip, becomes warm. Probably it will tingle.

When you have mastered this simple technique you can practise it when convenient. Practise in a quiet room. Close your eyes so that you can concentrate on the sound. Hum in your normal pitch as quietly as you can, concentrating on holding the pitch and bringing the sound forward. Then, being most careful not to change the pitch, gradually increase the power. This mastered, increase and decrease the power whilst still holding the constant pitch; this exercise is also excellent for enlarging the capacity to breathe. Repeat the exercise, first on a lower then on a higher note. Help yourself to succeed by visualising the stream of air ascending from the bottom of your lungs to the lips. Then occasionally let the lips very slightly open and close to test that they are held firmly but not tightly.

This will produce an 'M-M-M-M' sound. Later on, lessen the monotony by humming some music of a marked rhythm, always with a deliberate beat, never with the casualness normally associated with everyday humming.

Many speakers do not throw the voice forward and several speak right at the back of the throat; hence the special importance of this exercise. At first do it for three or four minutes at a time; and when it is mastered strive to keep up the custom for a couple of minutes daily. Relax as you practise it.

These exercises will help you develop the foundations for a good speaking voice – authoritative and friendly. Reading aloud is also a useful exercise. Imagine that you have an audience, and speak to bring out the meaning, and not just individual words. Finally, here is a simple exercise you can follow to help you create a better sounding image.

Relaxation Exercises

- *Head rolls*: Slowly rotate the head to the right, back around to the left, and forward. Do this five times, beginning at the right, and reverse five times, beginning at the left.
- *Shoulder rolls*: Rotate your right shoulder forward and leave it there for three seconds. Rotate your left shoulder forward, leaving it there for three seconds so that both your shoulders are forward. Next rotate your right shoulder back and then your left shoulder back so that both shoulders are back. Repeat this exercise ten times.
- *Facial relaxation*: Close your eyes. Then consciously relax your forehead, eyebrows, eyes, cheeks, nose, lips, jaws, ears

and neck, concentrating on each facial part for approximately five seconds. For the next twenty seconds visualise a relaxing fantasy.

No matter what type of speech you deliver, clear communication is an important skill. Here are some devices which will help clarify your communication.

- Use the outward breath and relax.
- Start positively and loudly.
- Let the pitch of your voice flow up and down the scale from high to low and back again, just as the pitch of a little child does when speaking.
- Use emphasis, pauses, inflections. Vary the pitch and volume. This will give light and shade to what you have to say.
- Use a warm and resonant voice. Avoid sounding harsh, too weak, too loud or flat. A monotonous voice is not interesting to listen to.
- Build your point vocally. Add emphasis and drama through the way you actually say your words by stressing the most important ones and shade the less important ones.
- Avoid 'uh' and 'um' and phrases such as 'okay' and 'you know'. Most speakers have the occasional one in their speech, but if you overdo this, the audience will begin to expect them and start counting.
- Make sufficient use of the pause.
- Make sure that your voice rises when you ask questions and falls when you make statements.
- Clearly articulate each sentence, phrase, word and syllable. Give full value to all the sounds in your speech.
- Display a lively amount of vocal energy. By making the words sound interesting you are more likely to have enthusiastic listeners.
- Make sure your thoughts forge ahead, helping to build up your argument.
- Have enough breath to finish each sentence on a strong note. Often 'ums' and 'ahs' are a result of insufficient breath. These sounds are often inserted to fill the void before

finishing a sentence or phrase.
- Use the rhetorical question to involve the audience; it also gives variety to your speech patterns.
- Vary your pitch, force, volume, rate and rhythm. Catch people's attention by getting noticeably louder at important points.
- Do not drop consonants.
- Use correct pronunciation. Many words have acceptable alternative pronunciations. In this case decide which one you will use – and be consistent throughout your speech.

If you observe good public speakers, you will almost certainly see that they are committed to their words. They show conviction and enthusiasm for what they say and how they say it.

PRONUNCIATION

Pronunciation is an important matter. In ordinary conversation the most common errors are due to carelessness. In public speaking, however, correct pronunciation is essential, because failure in this can expose the speaker to ridicule.

The general rule is that every letter and syllable in a word should be heard. It is unnecessary to refer here to variations in pronunciation due to dialect or accent. These are perfectly acceptable if genuine.

The following are some of the most common rules which are often broken by public speakers:

R is a letter often abused, and should not be sounded where it has no place. For example it is often wrongly used when a word ends in a vowel – 'idear', 'Indiar'.

W is sometimes substituted for the letter r, so that 'round' becomes 'wound', 'really' becomes 'weally'.

We sometimes encounter words that are new to us or that are part of a foreign language. A good dictionary will indicate the correct syllable emphasis, and therefore help with the pronunciation.

DELIVERY

Words Frequently Mispronounced

discipline	poignant	physicist
heinous	incomparable	advertisement
irreparable	dais	coiffure
viva-voce	faux-pas	February
mischievous	gist	feign
Diocesan	lamentable	precedent
superfluous	victuals	pronunciation

Pronunciation of difficult or unusual names can place the speaker in an embarrassing position. If you cannot find an immediate answer through reference books, the BBC or *Daily Telegraph* are useful resources for this type of enquiry.

Name	Pronunciation
Alnwick	Annick
Beaconsfield	Becconsfield
Beaulieu	Bewly
Bicester	Bister
Bromwich	Brumich
Brough	Bruff
Buccleuch	Bucklew
Cadogan	Caddugan
Cannes	Can
Charteris	Charters
Clough	Cluff
Cockburn	Co-burn
Cowper	Cooper
Derby	Darby
Drogheda	Droider
Farquhar	Farkwar
Goethe	Gerter
Herries	Harris
Home	Hume
Keighley	Kethley
Kerr	Carr
Marjoribanks	Marshbanks

McLeod	McCloud
Millais	Millay
Menzies	Mingies
Pepys	Peeps
Rabelais	Rablay
Sandys	Sands
Wemyss	Weems

Some General Rules

Doubled consonants are generally pronounced as single (e.g. beginner as begin-er) except in compound words with a prefix that can be used separately e.g. override.

The letter C: Before a, o, u, or any consonant except h, *c* is pronounced hard like *k*, and also when it is the last letter of a syllable, unless followed by e or i in the next syllable, e.g. calm, cone, cut, climb, romantic, social.

C is pronounced soft like *s* before e, i, or y, e.g. cell, cigar, and cygnet.

Ch: The usual pronunciation of *ch* is as in chance; but in words derived from the Greek it often has the sound of *k*, as in chasm. In words derived from French it is often pronounced *sh*, as in nonchalance. (The dictionary is useful for reference.)

The letter G is hard, as in gate, when it forms the last letter of a word, and in derivatives of words ending in g, e.g. dig, digger.

This is true almost without exception whether the g is doubled or not. It has the hard sound too before a, o, u, l and r when occurring in the same syllable as itself, and before e and i in words derived from Anglo-Saxon or German, e.g. gate, goat, gut, glance, grand, get, gift.

G is pronounced soft like *j* before e, i or y in words derived directly or indirectly from Latin, except when g is doubled before y, or the word is a derivative of one ending in g, when the rule given above is followed, e.g. general, gentle, margin, gypsum, baggy.

DELIVERY

USING THE MICROPHONE

As many speaking engagements involve large audiences, the use of a microphone is becoming increasingly common. When used correctly, the microphone can be an advantage.

Advantages

- The microphone is an excellent aid when speaking to very large audiences, e.g. conferences, particularly when wired to amplifying speakers around the hall. It ensures that everybody in the audience can hear.
- It is useful when you have to answer questions. With a hand-held or clip-on microphone you can walk around and out into your audience. If appropriate you could sit, and adopt a crisp conversational tone. In the after-dinner situation, you can stand behind your chair and use either a table microphone or one on a stand.
- Occasionally, the microphone is used where there is an overflow meeting, when many of the audience will be able to hear the speaker but not see him (for example a political meeting).

  In this case it would be a courtesy to both the speaker and the audience, if the speaker walks through the 'unsighted' rooms, and is perhaps introduced informally. It can also work for closed circuit television. This helps build a bridge between speaker and audience and smooths the way for the message to follow.
- The microphone is also useful at public meetings. It can help the chairman take and keep control if the situation is disruptive, and things are getting out of hand. The chairman has every right to gain control. It is a useful aid for dealing with hecklers.
- If a speaker wishes to speak in a relaxed, conversational manner to a large audience, he can remain seated for his speech and have the microphone placed about one foot away from him.

69

DELIVERY

Used correctly and with full rehearsal, there are few disadvantages to using the microphone. Remember that it is another technical detail which you have to check as part of your preparation. As a speaker you will encounter, and may have a choice of, the various types:

- Fixed on a stand which can be adjusted to the speaker's height.
- Fixed on a short stand or rest to place on a table.
- Attached to a lectern. It is often a good idea to have a microphone at each side of the lectern.
- Attached to a jacket or dress with a small clip – or hung around the neck. Advantageous if you wish to walk about. Because the microphone moves with you, you can do this without your voice fading. Be careful with this type of microphone that you don't get tangled in the wire.
- Hung from the ceiling. Height adjustable. The disadvantage is that these are static – usually set where the speaker will stand.

Often microphones will be a combination of the above. Increasingly popular with professional speakers is the cordless mike, and this has obvious advantages. One small disadvantage is that part of the apparatus has to be carried on you, so strong pockets are advisable.

Microphone Technique
Here are some hints for using the microphone.

- Whatever mike you choose, always practise with it first. The technique of using the microphone depends mainly on two considerations – the proper tone of voice and the proper distance.
- As to tone, increase your power rather than heighten your pitch. As a rough guide, imagine you are throwing your voice. Make use of control. When you begin speaking, watch the reaction of those sitting at the back of the room. Is their body language telling you it's too loud? I recently saw a

humorous example of this at a large wedding reception, when the guests put their hands over their ears when the bridegroom began his speech. Alternatively, are their faces strained?

- Rehearsing beforehand will solve these problems. This is particularly important if you are one of several speakers. The previous speaker may have adjusted the microphone to match his height, and that could leave you bending or stretching – either way it does not look professional, or comfortable. As to height, any position from just below the chin to the level of the chest should be suitable. The angle of the microphone, straight or tilted, and the relation of your position to the audience will decide your exact choice.
- If you wish to make an emphatic point, take a careful step back (almost rock back). This is a technique to avoid 'feedback'.
- Once you begin to speak, don't touch the microphone. If it squeals you may have accidentally touched it; take your hand away and it should stop. If you hear a loud popping sound from the mike, try adjusting it so that you are speaking into it at an angle instead of straight on.
- If several speakers are to appear on a panel to answer questions, a microphone each is advisable if the occasion is to flow smoothly. If only one mike is passed between them, continuity is lost.
- Always check that there is someone around with knowledge of the sound system. Don't rely on confident assurances along the lines of 'The system will be all right on the night.'
- Be aware of unguarded words in front of a live microphone; a mutter to the chairman that 'they were a dull lot' as you sit down may stifle your applause if the words boom out over the public address.
- Switch off noisy equipment, such as air conditioning fans or telephones, which may be a distraction.
- Don't fondle the microphone lead whilst you are talking.
- Avoid wearing nylon shirts and blouses. The instrument may crackle if it rests on a shirt front made of nylon.

- If it sounds wrong, then stop and have it adjusted before you continue. Stay calm, raise your voice and say for example: 'Will someone kindly switch on this wonderful piece of equipment?' With perseverance the engineer will come to your assistance. If it still plays up, then you will have to make the decision as to whether your voice will carry without the mike.
- Check with your audience. Say 'Can you hear me at the back?' If not, perhaps take a few steps forward, or adjust the position of the mike.

Experience will show you how to make best use of the microphone. Have the confidence to fall back on your own voice power if you need to.

THE MEDIA

If I possessed the power of conveying unlimited sexual
attraction through the potency of my voice, I would not
be reduced to accepting a miserable pittance from the
BBC for interviewing a faded female in a damp basement.
Gilbert Harding
(on being asked to sound more sexy
when interviewing Mae West)

One of the most rewarding results of giving speeches is that you can communicate with large numbers of people. If you are a specialist, or someone who has something of interest to say which has general appeal, you may be asked to speak on radio or television. Here you are likely to reach a very large audience. You may be asked to deliver a set talk, or perhaps you will be interviewed.

This can be as daunting as actually having to speak in front of a live audience, but the general technique of good speaking skills still apply. By now you will be familiar with the word 'preparation', and it is just as relevant for radio and television. In a television studio, the moment the cameras are turned on is fraught with tension. Fortunately very often the programmes are pre-recorded and any 'fluffs' will be edited out before the programme is shown at a later date.

Some Hints if You are Being Interviewed:

- The interviewer will generally give a few biographical details about you before he leads into the first question. Use this time to calm yourself. Take a deep breath before you answer. Avoid fillers such as, 'well', 'you know'.
- Forget the green eye of the live camera, the microphones, and the studio audience. Remember your conversational style, chat with the interviewer as if the two of you were on your own.
- Choose your words with care, don't criticise others.
- Take time to formulate your answer and try not to be intimidated into responding before you are ready.

If Delivering a Set Speech:

- You will probably be asked to provide a copy of the speech before you deliver it. The studio will then put it on to the autocue.
- The autocue should be read at your normal rate of speech, and again the tone should be conversational.

The radio or television interviewer will give you the general theme of the interview, but may not give you any indication of specific questions. (Many feel that if the interviewee knows the questions, spontaneity will be lost when the questions are answered.) You may be asked to attend the studio for a rehearsal, and your voice will be tested if you have not broadcast before.

If you are asked to appear on television, the station will advise you about what colours to wear etc. Select something from your wardrobe that reflects your professional image and with which you are comfortable. When you arrive at the station, you will be shown into the Green Room where you will be advised of the procedure. The station make-up artist will make you up for cameras.

A Radio Interview May be Done:

- In a recording studio, where the interviewer sits opposite the person being interviewed.
- As a telephone interview, where the interview is conducted over the telephone. The radio station will telephone you just before you are due to 'go live'.
- In a self-operating studio. These are often used by small local stations. Operation is generally fairly simple, and the interview is conducted with the interviewee speaking into a microphone.

Radio stations in particular are usually very helpful in putting interviewees at ease. The interviewer or assistant will generally call a few days before the intended interview to discuss the subject briefly. Over the last few years, I have given many radio interviews. Here are a few hints from my own experience which may be helpful.

The most important thing for me is to get off to a good start, i.e. to answer the first question with confidence.

- Agree with the interviewer what the first question will be. (I find that if this goes well, the tone is set for the remainder of the interview.)
- In the light of the discussion that I have had with the interviewer earlier, I prepare some answers. Using the same rules as when preparing speech cue cards, I use key words to jog my memory. Very often I don't need to use these notes, but they are useful to fall back on should you dry up. They are particularly useful if you have to give statistics, quote from reports etc. when it is important that the information is accurate.

DELIVERY

- Inject some enthusiasm into your voice. Be positive, never knock the opposition.

And some good advice from the actress, Joanna Lumley:

Relax and enjoy yourself. Remember people are only people.

Preparation Summaries

Good Openings

- Begin with a vivid personal illustration of your theme.
- Use a quotation or historical fact that sums up your topic.
- Show your audience you are one of them – build empathy.
- Shock them. Begin with some shocking facts or statistics.
- Amuse them. Begin with a joke/historical illustration of their current dilemma.

Keep Them Listening

- Use logical argument.
- Give dramatic illustrations of the points you make.
- Keep it simple and punchy.
- Avoid boring lists.
- Keep to your prepared speech.
- Be specific, not general.
- Give personal examples and anecdotes.
- Consider opposing points of view.
- Draw your evidence together for the conclusion.

Successful Endings

- Reaffirm the main thrust of your speech.
- End with your rallying cry.
- Pose a teasing question – throw the debate to the audience.
- Sum up opposing arguments.
- Suggest solutions.

- Relevant quotation.
- Humorous story.
- End on a positive/optimistic note.

Tips for Script Writing

- Stick to plain English, and make it grammatically correct. Avoid unnecessary qualifying words such as 'very', 'really', 'awfully', 'hopefully'. As a result, statements will have more impact.
- As your speech is meant to be heard and not read, use conversational English. Avoid grandiose or long-winded turns of phrase. Use short, simple words.
- Avoid archaic expressions, such as 'please be upstanding'.
- Avoid using phrases where one word will do. For example use 'now' instead of the cliché 'at this point in time'.
- Avoid slang, clichés, jargon and swear words.
- Use positive verbs positively. Instead of saying, 'He was not happy with the report', say, 'He was unhappy with the report.' Even though you are making a negative statement, you are using a positive verb. This makes the sentence stronger.
- Keep in mind your audience, objectives, and timing as you edit your script. Keep it short and punchy.
- If appropriate, always add some humour.
- Prepare your script so that you can read it easily, allowing for good audience eye contact – mark it appropriately.
- Rehearse your speech out loud. Build in movement and gestures where applicable.

Tips for Editing

- Be ruthless. Delete everything in your draft that is unsuitable. Edit keeping the 'must' rule in mind.
- Be precise in your choice of words.
- Rewrite any sentences or phrases that sound unnatural.
- Work your script until the words trip off your tongue. Aim for a smooth flow.

- Check that it doesn't run over time.
- Rehearse several times and make adjustments until you feel it is as good as you can get it.

Tips for Using Humour

- Keep a file of funny stories and jokes.
- Begin with a good joke to break the audience in.
- Keep jokes relevant.
- Consider your audience and never tell an offensive or hurtful joke.
- Make the butt of the joke someone the audience knows, but adhere to the above.
- Laugh with them, not at them.
- A joke at your own expense will always raise a laugh.
- One-liners are safer bets than lengthy stories.
- Gauge the sense of humour of your audience by their response to the jokes of previous speakers.
- Leave out any jokes you think won't appeal.

Delivering Humour

- Smile – look and stand confidently.
- Get your timing right.
- Make use of the dramatic pause to build up suspense.
- Put your stress on the key words of the joke and accompany them with plenty of expression.
- Hold the pause a little longer than normal when delivering the punch line.

Tips for Good Audience Rapport

- Be considerate in the way you speak; make sure that you can be seen, heard and understood.
- Use humour to show your sympathy and gain theirs.
- Establish eye contact with all of them.
- Have a conversation with them – Talk 'to' your audience, not 'at' or 'down to' them.

PREPARATION SUMMARIES

- Involve them.
- Earn their respect:
  - Be well prepared
  - Address their needs
  - Look and sound happy to be there
  - Dress smartly – appropriately to the occasion.

Adapt the speeches and toasts in the following chapter to suit your purposes.

Social Toasts and Speeches

THE LOYAL TOAST

No speech is required. This is normally the first and main toast. The Chairman simply says:

Ladies and Gentlemen – The Queen!

There is no smoking until after the Loyal Toast(s) have been made. Immediately after them, the chairman should announce:

Ladies and Gentlemen, you may smoke.

Less commonly, there may be a second toast. The second Loyal Toast, if proposed, must immediately follow the first. Again no speech is required. This toast is to the other members of the Royal Family. This second Loyal Toast may be slightly varied.

Ladies and Gentlemen, I have the honour to propose the toast of (e.g.) 'Queen Elizabeth, the Queen Mother, The Prince Philip, Duke of Edinburgh, The Prince of Wales – and other members of the Royal Family.'

The Chairman should ascertain the correct form beforehand. This is issued officially with the approval of the Queen.

GRACE

To avoid upsetting any particular religious groups a layman may sometimes be asked to say 'grace' before a dinner.

For the food we are about to receive may we be truly thankful, Amen

This would probably be acceptable in most cases. Whatever form of grace you say keep it short and avoid humour as well as Latin words which may not be understood by everyone present.

TOAST TO THE LADIES

This toast is usually (but not necessarily) proposed by a bachelor in the company.

Often the youngest or oldest bachelor is chosen; the spirit of this choice should be reflected in his speech. This type of toast should always be light-hearted and flattering to the women, and care should be taken to include jokes and anecdotes which reflect good taste. Depending on the audience, 'Ladies' may be substituted by 'Women'.

Gentlemen,
The pleasure of proposing this toast has been given to me because I happen to be the oldest bachelor here this evening.

I hope that you will not think that because I am single, I know nothing about the ladies. I have not, of course, the same detailed experience as my married friends, but I look forward to that later. Meanwhile I am steadily increasing my knowledge of the ladies, at least, to the extent that they will allow me. I relish every new piece of knowledge gained, and this only serves to increase my admiration.

Today, we often hear talk of equal opportunity between the sexes. I believe this has never existed and never will. Margaret Thatcher was right when she said 'Once a woman is made man's equal, she becomes his superior.' Gentlemen, women have never been our equals; they have *always* been vastly superior to us.

Let the ladies remain as feminine and irresistible as they are now. I ask you to join me in drinking to the health of all our lovely ladies – *Vive la différence*.

Gentlemen – the Ladies!

Reply

Gentlemen,

My difficulty in reply to your most generous toast is that I am not allowed to express my true thoughts out loud. I am supposed to thank you for your kind words with modesty.

I did agree with your assessment of the subject of equality. Margaret Thatcher was right, we *are* superior. However, that is not to say that the men in our lives are left out or in any way inferior. Denis, her husband, was once asked: 'Who wears the trousers in your house?' His reply – 'I do, and I wash and iron them as well.' You see, gentlemen, that is true equality!

After that remark, you may be surprised when I tell you that I have been an admirer of men almost from birth. I have always found you delightful companions and charming company for all occasions.

Gentlemen, I think you're wonderful!

Quotations

WOMEN

A woman can look both moral and exciting . . . if she also looks as if it was quite a struggle.

Edna Ferber

There are three intolerable things in life – cold coffee, luke-warm champagne, and overexcited women.

Orson Welles

SOCIAL TOASTS AND SPEECHES

A woman uses her intelligence to find reasons to support her intuition.

G.K. Chesterton

Women are most fascinating between the ages of thirty-five and forty, after they have won a few races and know how to pace themselves. Since few ever pass forty, maximum fascination can continue indefinitely.

Christian Dior

Women should be obscene and not heard.

John Lennon

It was a woman who drove me to drink, and I never had the courtesy to thank her for it.

W.C. Fields

MEN

His mother should have thrown him away and kept the stork.

Mae West

Giving a man space is like giving a dog a computer: the chances are he will not use it wisely.

Bette-Jane Raphael

No nice men are good at getting taxis.

Katharine Whitehorn

Whenever I date a man, I think, is this the man I want my children to spend their weekends with?

Rita Rudner

Some of my best leading men have been horses and gods.

Elizabeth Taylor

Wedding Speeches

GENERAL ADVICE

Speeches play an important role at weddings. The nice thing about this occasion is that you can be sure that the guests are on your side. They want your speech to be a success. Wedding speeches vary according to the tone of the event, i.e. whether it is a formal or informal affair. This will also include the accepted customs of perhaps different religions and cultures.

Weddings are joyful occasions and the main aim of your speech should be to unify the guests so that they feel they are part of the celebrations. A light-hearted approach is most appropriate for this occasion. Humour creates a friendly and relaxed atmosphere; a welcome ingredient in any wedding speech.

Many speakers feel uncomfortable using original humour or anecdotes. If you feel that this doesn't suit your style of delivery, then use one of the many other devices available to you. For example, carefully chosen quotations from famous people are sure to get at least a chuckle. If you have time for research, then your local library is a mine of useful information. Film stars and other well-known personalities are great sources of quotations about marriage, most having attended several of their own. Turn to the back of the book for some quotable quotes on marriage. Another idea is to research historical events which took place on the same date as the wedding.

To most people, humour does not come easily, so don't waste time agonising over funny one-liners. Concentrate on being sincere. Remember the purpose of the wedding speech is to give thanks, good wishes to the newlyweds and praise where due. Your thanks should include the hosts and other organisers as well as honouring the bride and groom and acknowledging the presence of any special guests. Following the rules of etiquette at a formal wedding will make sure that nobody will be offended or left out.

Many people consider large formal weddings to be an organisational nightmare. Certainly they require a lot of careful planning. The success of the day will depend on the amount of hard work behind the scenes. The same applies to speeches. Always start your preparations well ahead of time.

Purpose of the Speeches

Once the leading men have agreed to deliver the traditional speeches, they should start preparation immediately. The speaker should fix in his mind the objective or purpose, which is to thank people, propose toasts, or reply to other speeches. Most speakers will also want to entertain the guests, and this is therefore a good time to select appropriate material such as anecdotes.

There are no hard and fast rules on who may speak at the wedding, but traditionally, the groom, best man and bride's father will make the speeches. It is also becoming increasingly common for the ladies to have their say, for example the bride and bride's mother. Recently, a friend's father died just before her marriage, and the groom's father, her future father-in-law, stepped in to help.

Many people feel that they are just too nervous to speak in front of an audience, and in this case, an uncle or brother can give the speech. There is no use insisting on convention if it is going to ruin the enjoyment of the day.

Everybody is nervous about making a speech, but preparation is the key. The following information will answer some of the questions you may have about the conventions of wedding speeches:

Who Introduces the Speeches?

If there is no toastmaster, the best man performs these duties. He judges when the speeches should start, perhaps as the guests are finishing the dessert course of their meal. He then calls each speaker in turn.

Order of Speakers
There are at least three speakers who will rise in the following order:

- The bride's father.
- The groom.
- The best man.

It is probably better to avoid ready-made speeches. Many speakers make the mistake of delivering a ready-made speech in parrot fashion, which doesn't sound sincere. Try and write the speech yourself. Using your own words and phrases will make your speech sound as if it comes from the heart. That is not to say that you can't use ideas and outlines from this or any other book on speech-making. It should be just that – an outline to which you add your personal touches.

PLANNING CHECKLIST

Timing
How long will the speech last? Remember quality is better than quantity. Many good speeches have been ruined by the speaker elaborating on every incident from the bride's past. This is not necessary, a few well-chosen anecdotes will suffice. Plan to speak for between five and ten minutes, perhaps a little longer for a very formal occasion. This will ensure that the guests will not get bored.

There are four main things to consider when thinking about the wedding speech:

THEME
Begin your research by setting yourself a theme. For example, sharing.

RESEARCH
Collect anecdotes about the bride and groom by talking to their

friends and family. Most guests will be interested in this topic and are sure to sit up and listen.

EMPATHY
Try not to exclude your audience. Avoid too much of 'I remember when . . .' Use the more general phrase 'I am told that . . .' This will make all the guests feel at ease and will help build the essential ingredient for all good speeches – a warm rapport with your audience.

OVER PREPARING
Don't overdo it. Some speakers find that they invest so much time and energy on the research that they run out of time to write and rehearse the speech.

A general rule for all speeches is: *keep it simple and to the point*!

Writing the Speech
A wedding speech should reflect both the personality of the speaker and the tone of the occasion. The key is to be yourself and let your personality show through.

Here are some useful guidelines for putting your speech together.

- Work through your notes and select the bits you intend to keep. A highlighter pen is useful for this purpose.
- Once editing is complete, arrange the information in order, chronologically or otherwise.
- Make a list of the thanks, the toast, and any other important points that must be included in your speech.
- Begin by deciding your opening remarks. Don't worry if you spend a fair amount of time on this. As stated in previous chapters, a good opening is the key for memorable speeches. Once you have a good opening, the rest of the speech will flow on and everything should fall into place.
- Strive to be positive. Avoid writing anything negative about the bride or groom. It is well to remember the old adage here: if in doubt, leave it out.

- On no account include any rude jokes or sexual innuendoes, as they are usually not appreciated. When you fail to raise a response, the guests will feel embarrassed and you will pray for the floor to open and swallow you up. Once you have lost your audience in this way it is difficult to recover.
- Write your speech as if you were talking to a friend. Conversational style is acceptable for all occasions. Avoid using long words and sentences, and prepare your notes as suggested earlier.

THE FATHER OF THE BRIDE

The bride's father might order his speech in the following way.

ABOUT HIS DAUGHTER
He might begin by talking about the happiness he and his wife experienced in bringing up such a fine daughter. This will give him the opportunity to relate a few stories about her early life. Perhaps he will continue with some amusing anecdotes leading up to when she met her future husband.

WELCOMING THE NEW SON-IN-LAW
This will give him the opportunity of welcoming his new son-in-law. He might reflect on the loss of a daughter, and welcome her new husband to the family circle.

FATHERLY ADVICE
The father's speech should not be heavy-handed, but as it is a semi-serious occasion, he may wish to offer some words of advice to the newlyweds, perhaps using a quotation: 'Almost all married people fight, although many are ashamed to admit it. Actually a marriage in which no quarrelling at all takes place may well be one that is dead or dying from emotional undernourishment. If you care, you probably fight.'

WEDDING SPEECHES

Checklist

THE FATHER'S SPEECH SHOULD INCLUDE

- His happiness in bringing up his daughter.
- One or two stories, possibly funny, which illustrate her character.
- His daughter beginning her new life.
- Welcome to his son-in-law and his parents as new members of the family.
- Advice on the couple's future together.

The bride's father then proposes the first toast to the bride and groom. Traditionally, everyone stands for the toast – except the people being toasted.

THE GROOM

The groom should now respond to the toast. His speech is mainly to thank people, and so he is not expected to deliver a long or entertaining address.

Checklist

THE GROOM SHOULD THANK

- The M.C. and the first speaker.
- Both sets of parents.
- The best man, the guests and the people who arranged the flowers and cake for their help.
- His own parents (he may at this point present a gift or bouquet of flowers to his own and the bride's mother).
- His wife for marrying him.

THE GROOM THEN PROPOSES

- A toast to 'absent friends'.
- Finally a toast to the bridesmaids.

WEDDING SPEECHES

THE BEST MAN

The best man has the hardest job of all in terms of speeches since he is allowed, and therefore expected, to show a certain licence to portray the groom in an amusing light.

The first duty the best man has to perform in his speech is to thank the groom for his kind words and toast to the bridesmaids on their behalf. Telegrams are often read at this point. The best man should then deliver a light-hearted speech and end it by toasting the newlyweds.

ADAPTING JOKES

Aim to entertain, not offend. If the anecdote is amusing but rather negative, tell it and then disassociate yourself from the views it expresses. For example, supposing you want to refer to the fact that the groom is a medical student and you have a story about a king dying in the Middle Ages who says the physician has killed him, tell this story but end it, 'Of course medicine has come a long way since those days.'

You could always refer the story to other people. For example, if you wanted to use the line, 'doctors bury their mistakes' without appearing to criticise the bridegroom who is a medical student or doctor, you could say instead that 'other doctors bury their mistakes'.

TOAST TO ABSENT FRIENDS

This speech should be short and sincere.

Ladies and Gentlemen,
   You do not want a long speech to introduce this toast. It is a simple toast, with a wealth of meaning. Most of us have family and loved ones who cannot be with us tonight. Their presence here would add to the enjoyment of our festivities. But I am sure that they would want us to enjoy ourselves in

their absence. Let us take a brief pause to think of them for a few moments, and drink in silence to – Absent Friends.

SAMPLE SPEECHES

The following sample speeches can be adapted to suit different situations and speakers. Choose the most appropriate for your purpose and substitute your own details.

After each section I have included some relevant quotations. A further selection can be found at the end of the book.

No. 1
Toast to the Bride and Groom
(BRIEF TOAST AT AN INFORMAL WEDDING PARTY)

I would like to propose a toast to ——— and ———, wishing them much joy and happiness for their future together. A perfect match.

——— and ———.

No. 2
Toast to the Bride and Groom
(SUITABLE FOR AN OLDER MAN ADDRESSING A LARGE, DISTINGUISHED AUDIENCE)

Ladies and Gentlemen,

It is always a pleasure to attend a wedding. They say that the world loves a lover and I think this is true. Marriage is the expression of love, and also the start of a lifelong adventure. Plato said, 'The beginning is the most important part of the work.' If that is the case, then ——— and ——— have been fortunate in enjoying the most wonderful beginning. They already have most of the good gifts one would wish upon a young couple. ——— is a beautiful bride, ——— is a handsome husband, and both come from secure family homes where their parents have set examples of what a good marriage should be.

91

A good marriage is not something you can create on your own without help from your partner. It is a joint venture. Marriage is like a journey in a boat. You cannot drill a hole in the boat and when water floods in say to your companion, 'It's nothing to do with you, the water is coming in on my side of the boat.' You must row in the same direction. If marriage is a boat, then many of us are in the same boat!

———— and ————, you are embarking on a wonderful journey, and you have many friends who will support you, and help you, and wish you well. I would now like to ask everyone in this room to stand with me and raise their glasses.

(Pause briefly until the guests are standing.)

I propose a toast to the long life, health, wealth, and happy marriage, of ———— and ————.

To ———— and ————!

No. 3

(A BRIEF, SIMPLE, DIRECT SPEECH FOR THE BRIDE'S FATHER)

Reverend ————, Ladies and Gentlemen, all my guests,

I cannot tell you how pleased I am today to see my daughter ———— looking so radiantly happy, as she begins life as the wife of ————. My wife and I do not feel that we are losing ————, but entrusting her to ————'s good care. During the last few months as we have got to know him better, he has shown himself to be exactly the sort of person we had hoped ———— would marry – charming, sincere, and reliable – with a clear idea of what he wants from life and how to achieve it.

I know that his many friends and family think that they make an attractive couple, and will want to join me in wishing ———— and ———— a long and happy married life together. So please stand and raise your glasses, and drink to the health and happiness of ———— and ————.

(Pause.)

To ———— and ————.

92

No. 4

(RELATIVE'S/FRIEND'S SPEECH WHEN THE BRIDE'S FATHER IS
RECENTLY DECEASED)

It is my great pleasure to be here with you on this happy
occasion and to help ——— and ——— celebrate their
marriage. I have known ——— and her parents for many
years, since I/we/they came to London/Cardiff/Edinburgh.
———'s late father, ——— used to enjoy a game of golf/
cricket/rugby, and we spent many happy hours together
sailing/relaxing often accompanied by ———,

I remember ——— saying that ——— seemed to be a very
pleasant/good-natured/ambitious young man. I know that
——— and ——— got on well, and ——— would have been
delighted to have seen this happy day. Although we miss
———'s presence, and his unfailing good humour, we know
that he was looking forward to this wedding and we have
fulfilled his hopes and wishes, and in a sense he is with us
here today in our happy memories of him. He would have
been very satisfied to know what a comfort ——— has been
to our family, how understanding, how supportive a friend in
time of need. He has been a tower of strength to ———. It
was ———'s express wish that ——— and ———'s wedding
should go ahead as planned.

———, your father would be proud of you today, as I'm
sure ——— is. And it is with every confidence that I tell you I
am sure that this young couple will have a very happy
marriage, and I would ask you to join me in wishing them
both a long, happy, and prosperous future together.

Please stand and lift your glasses. I propose a toast – to
——— and ———.

(Lift glass in air and wait for everybody to stand and raise
glasses.)

To ——— and ———.

No. 5

Father's Toast to Bride and Groom
(BRIDE A JUNIOR SCHOOL TEACHER)

It seems to me that many people enter the teaching profession because they genuinely love children. ——— was a 'natural' for teaching the young. This is where she can be bossy if she likes with impunity. It's gratifying for ——— and myself to know that ——— works amongst the children that she loves. Her constant daily practice in managing little ones will stand her in good stead in her own family future, not that we anticipate her having thirty children all about the same age.

That reminds me of a young lady teacher in a railway carriage who was fairly certain that she recognised the man sitting opposite as the parent of a child in her class. She said to him, 'Excuse me, but aren't you the father of one of my children?' . . . He said, 'No, but can I put my name down?'

Ambiguities constantly cause misunderstandings in children's minds. A minor example is that of the little boy who was asked in a mental arithmetic session, 'What's seven times fifteen?' He said, 'A hundred and five.' The teacher said, 'Very good!' The boy said, 'What do you mean – "very good"? It's perfect.'

Then there was the occasion concerning a little girl and her playmate called David (the name has been changed to protect the innocent). She said to her Mummy, 'Me and David had "secs" again at dinner time.' Her horrified Mummy said 'What do you mean, "sex"?' The little girl said, 'You know, "seconds". If there's any dinner or pudding left over, some of us get a second helping.'

———, you will already have heard from ——— quite a few tales about teaching the young. ——— and I used to enjoy an almost daily ration of these, and you can look forward to them as a constant source of amusement. It will compensate for irksome little things that happen when ——— forgets she's not in the classroom, and you get a clip round the ear for mislaying your pen.

Come what may, ——, —— and I have great pleasure in welcoming you into our family. As far as any advice goes that I can offer to you both, —— and ——, in your married state, perhaps I should follow up what I've said about —— forgetting that she's not at school, when she's with you ——. ——, —— is a big boy now. Don't embarrass him in front of dinner guests by correcting the way he uses his knife and fork.

——, for your part, to keep the harmony play safe and do such things as standing up and saying, 'Good morning, Miss' at the start of each day.

Ladies and gentlemen, I should like to propose a toast to our happy couple for their continuing happiness. Would you raise your glasses please, and drink to the health and happiness of —— and ——.

No. 6

(BRIDE'S GRANDFATHER, FATHER ILL)

It's difficult for me to say that it's a pleasure to make this speech. ——'s unfortunate illness has deprived him of his joyful privilege. What a pity! How proud he would have been, escorting —— to the altar. On behalf of all of us I send out thoughts to him for a speedy recovery. He'll naturally be visualising what's going on here and be with us in spirit. I ask —— especially to bear this in mind, so that her heart will be lighter about her Dad's physical absence.

In the short time that's been available to me to prepare a speech in ——'s place, I've tried to conjecture what he would have said about ——, and also what he wouldn't say. Let me explain what I mean by that last remark before you get the wrong idea. When someone is very close to you, it can be a matter of not seeing the wood for the trees. A salient aspect of their character comes to be taken so much for granted that you lose conscious sight of it.

I suspect something about —— that her Dad would have overlooked because, to use a different metaphor, it was too much under his nose. It's common enough to hear a person

95

described as having a bright and cheery disposition. Thank goodness that there is a generous scattering of such people, because they cheer us up by the briefest of encounters.

Now, ———, is one of that kind, but something more. She looks on the bright side of things. She believes that every cloud has a silver lining. I remember one sunny day in spring when there was a prolonged shower. There was a job my son and I wanted to do in the garden that required the ground to be dry. My son said 'Don't worry. The rain's drying up as fast as it's coming down.' I said, 'The trouble is, it's coming down as fast as it's drying up.' That illustrates the two directly opposite ways of looking at the same thing.

We can, furthermore, be quite simply mistaken in our view of a situation, like the chap who was called up for the army during the war. He said to them, 'It's no good you having me. I have one leg shorter than the other.' They said, 'That's all right. The ground where you're going's uneven.'

I've tried to point out that being a jolly person and looking on the bright side do not have to go hand in hand. A quiet person can still be one who looks on the bright side. But when the two are combined, and combined in such a lovely girl as ———, what a delight we have!

———, if you've been listening carefully, perhaps you'll have appreciated something more about ———'s worth. Incidentally, ———, I'd hate you or your parents to get the idea that you're considered of small importance in the scheme of things. I've naturally spoken warmly of my lovely granddaughter, because that's what her father would have been expected to do. I could go on and on about her. In fact, a lot of people do go on about her, but that's another matter.

I know you more by reputation than the pleasure of personal contact, ———. Happily, now that you're permanently installed in our family there will be more scope for that pleasure. There's one warning I must give you, though. You've a high reputation to live up to.

———, you and your family are gladly welcomed into ———'s family, and ——— and ——— want everyone present to be thanked for taking part in this celebration.

I would ask you all now to join me, please, in the toast to the happy couple, —— and ——.

No. 7
Toast to Bride and Groom (Second Marriage)
(SHORT SPEECH FOR A BRIDE ENJOYING HER FIRST MARRIAGE TO A DIVORCED MAN)

——, for you this is a first marriage and a time of excitement and hope. For —— it is a second marriage. He liked marriage so much that despite all the difficulties of his first attempt, when he met you he decided to try it again.

——, you may not realise it, but you are gaining the advantage of marrying a man who has had the sharp corners rubbed off him. A mature specimen. A vintage blend.

——, I'd just like to remind you that for every man that speaks from experience there's a wife who isn't listening.

We hope that you will always enjoy life together, a very long and happy life together, and that you will always retain the enthusiasm of this new start, and remember the joy and delight of finding each other, which is so evident today.

So we will all raise our glasses to you and toast your future. To —— and ——.

No. 8
Toast to Bride and Groom
(SHORT, HAPPY, SLIGHTLY HUMOROUS SPEECH WHEN THE GROOM IS MARRYING FOR THE FIRST TIME TO A DIVORCED WOMAN)

——, for you this is a first marriage and a time of expectation and hope. For —— it is a second marriage. You must be especially proud today, because she liked you so much that despite all the difficulties of her first marriage, when she met you she decided to try it again. What an honour!

——, you have the advantage of experience. ——, you may not realise it, but you are gaining many advantages by marrying a mature woman. Vintage.

Advice to the groom? Easy. When ——— hands you a dishcloth, blow your nose on it and hand it back.

We hope that both of you will always enjoy married life, a very long and happy life together. And that you will always retain the enthusiasm of this new start, and remember the joy and delight of finding each other, which is so evident today. So we will all raise our glasses to you and toast to your future.

To ——— and ———.

No. 9
Best Man's Toast to Bride and Groom
(VERY SMALL INFORMAL WEDDING – NO BRIDESMAIDS)

This is a lovely, small, intimate gathering of friends, which is just as ——— and ——— wanted it to be. How honoured we are to have been chosen to share this very special occasion with them.

Everyone here is a close friend or relative and we all have personal knowledge of ———'s unique qualities, her kindness, her sense of humour, her loyal friendship. And we are delighted that she is marrying ———, who is admired/loved by his family and close friends and is respected by all of us for his kindness/loyalty/talents/ zest for life. They make a perfect couple and share many good qualities and they both deserve all the good things in life.

So let's wish them both a very happy married life together. Has everyone got a drink? Good.

To ——— and ———.

No. 10
Toast to the Bride's Parents
(GROOM'S SPEECH, REPLYING TO FIRST TOAST TO BRIDE AND GROOM)

Reverend ———, Ladies and Gentlemen, (Pause).

Thank you so very much ——— for those kind words. It

goes almost without saying how pleased I am to be here today. I intend to speak only for a few minutes, as I know that there are other people who would like to say a few words.

As you know ——— has been a much sought-after young woman, and I am delighted that today I have won the first prize.

My new mother-in-law, ———, has worked long and hard for many months to make this day a success. All the little details such as these beautiful floral arrangements/cake decorations/bridesmaids' dresses were planned by her, and my father-in-law, ——— has taken on his second mortgage without complaint. I am very happy and privileged to be part of ———'s family, and to know that my parents feel the same. Speaking of whom, today represents a great occasion for both my parents, being the culmination of many years of planning of a different sort. They have supported me through university, taught me the difference between right and wrong, so that I know which I am enjoying at any given time!

——— is beautiful, intelligent and ambitious. The list of her good qualities is extremely long. Unfortunately I cannot read her handwriting. I would like to thank you all for your presence, particularly ———, who has travelled all the way from ——— for this occasion, and we are delighted that ———'s sister ——— flew all the way from ——— to be such a charming bridesmaid. Of course she had a little help from ——— and ———, who looked so sweet holding ———'s train.

My best man, ———, has made everything go smoothly, and made his contribution to what has seemed the perfect day.

ALTERNATIVE ENDING

Finally, I must pay tribute to the bridesmaids ——— and ——— whose invaluable support has helped to make this day so successful.

IF THERE ARE NO BRIDESMAIDS, THE TOAST TO HIS
PARENTS-IN-LAW AS FOLLOWS

In conclusion, thank you, everybody, for listening and I hope
you are having a wonderful afternoon/evening and are all as
happy as we are today.

Would you kindly stand and raise your glasses and drink a
toast to the health of your hosts, two wonderful people,
——— and ——— (Pause).

To ——— and ———.

No. 11

Toast to Bridegroom and Both Families
(INFORMAL TOAST BY THE BRIDE)

I'd like to propose a toast to the most wonderful man in the
world, my new husband, ———. I'd like to thank his parents
for what they have contributed over the years to make him
the person he is, supporting him through university, and also
for making me such a welcome member of their family. I
must also thank my parents for everything they have done for
me and especially this wonderful event, my wedding to
———.

May we all meet on many more happy occasions.

To ———.

No. 12

(TOAST TO THE BRIDE AND GROOM BY BEST MAN OR FRIEND
OF THE COUPLE)

A couple had been courting for some forty years. Each
evening he would call at her home. She would serve him
dinner and then they would sit together watching television
until it was time for him to take his leave. On the fortieth
anniversary of their meeting, the same routine was followed: evening meal, television and the couple sitting
silently in the same room. Suddenly, the woman said to the
man, 'What about us getting married?' To which the man

replied, 'What, us? Who would have us at our age?'

I am delighted, ladies and gentlemen, that our delightful couple here today have not kept us waiting quite so long. Particularly so, because I would have been most upset to have been denied the privilege and honour of proposing their health.

Both ——— and ——— are known to us all for their impeccable good taste. I doubt if they have ever illustrated this better than by their choice of each other as life partners.

It is customary to wish the bride and groom a happy life together. To my mind, there is no doubt that this will most certainly be the case with ——— and ———, because they will work at making it so and, as with everything else they have embarked on, they will succeed.

Ladies and gentlemen, will you please stand up and drink the toast to our charming couple; may they enjoy health, happiness and long life.

No. 13
Response of the Bridegroom

Mr ———, Ladies and Gentlemen,

My wife and I are beginning our wedded life with an agreement – the agreement being our most grateful thanks to you, Mr ———, for the very kind and pleasant manner in which you have proposed our health, and to you all for the hearty manner in which you have responded to the good wishes so eloquently expressed by our friend.

I do not deserve the good things that have been said of me, but I will try to live up to them, and to be worthy of my wife.

In conclusion let me again say that I greatly appreciate your kindness, and my wife – you see I am getting used to her new title – wishes me to thank you most heartily for your good wishes. I am sincerely grateful to you all for your kindness in drinking our health.

WEDDING SPEECHES

Quotations

WEDDINGS/MARRIAGE

Of all actions of a man's life his marriage does least concern other people; yet of all actions of our life it is more meddled with by other people.

John Sleden

If it were not for the presents, an elopement would be preferable.

George Ade

It has been said that a bride's attitude towards her betrothed can be summed up in three words: aisle, altar, hymn.

Frank Muir

The Wedding March always reminds me of the music played when soldiers go into battle.

Heinrich Heine

Marriage is a great institution, but I'm not ready for an institution yet.

Mae West

Marriage is a great invention; but then again, so is a bicycle repair kit.

Billy Connolly

Marriage is not all bed and breakfast.

Noel Coward

A man in love is incomplete until he is married. Then he is finished.

Zsa Zsa Gabor

WEDDING SPEECHES

The chain of wedlock is so heavy that it takes two to carry it – sometimes three.

Alexandre Dumas

A certain sort of talent is indispensable for people who would spend years together and not bore themselves to death.

Robert Louis Stevenson

It is a woman's business to get married as soon as possible and a man's to keep unmarried as long as he can.

George Bernard Shaw

Marriage is popular because it combines the maximum of temptation with the maximum of opportunity.

George Bernard Shaw

I chose my wife, as she did her wedding gown, for qualities that would wear well.

Oliver Goldsmith

SECOND MARRIAGE

To lose one husband is a misfortune. To lose two looks like carelessness.

Jane Austen

Many a man owes his success to his first wife and his second wife to his success.

Jim Backus

The triumph of hope over experience.

Dr Samuel Johnson

We're number two. We try harder.

Avis Car Rental advertisement

When widows exclaim loudly against second marriages, I would always lay a wager that the man, if not the wedding day, is absolutely fixed on.

Henry Fielding

HUSBANDS

The most labour saving device today is still a husband with money.

Joey Adams

A husband is what is left of a man after the nerve is extracted.

Helen Rowland

An archaeologist is the best husband any woman can have; the older she gets, the more interested he is in her.

Agatha Christie

WIVES

The trouble with my wife is that she is a whore in the kitchen and a cook in bed.

Geoffrey Gorer

Wives are young men's mistresses, companions for middle age, and old men's nurses.

Francis Bacon

When a man opens a car door for his wife, it's either a new car or a new wife.

Prince Philip

There are lots of good women who, when they get to heaven, will watch to see if the Lord goes out nights.

Ed Howe

Anniversary and Birthday Toasts

WEDDING ANNIVERSARY

An anniversary celebration should be just that – a celebration.

This is an occasion where it is quite usual for a longer speech than you would perhaps give for a wedding or christening speech. This will be a sentimental, romantic event, and you should take your tone from the occasion.

By now you will be familiar with the word *planning*. For this particular type of speech thorough research should take priority. Guests will want to hear about a couple's long married life together. Younger members of the extended family will also be curious.

Checklist
Speak to the couple's old friends. The answers to the following questions will form the basis for your speech.

- How did they meet?
- What were their first impressions of one another?
- Where and when did they marry?
- Have they ever separated for long periods of time?
- Did they write love letters to each other?
- Is there anyone attending the celebration who was present at the wedding?
- Where did they attend school, college, university?
- What careers did they follow?
- Any notable achievements, personal, academic, professional?

105

- The family, children, grandchildren, great-grandchildren. This may be one of the few occasions when the extended family get together. Be sure not to miss anyone out, by writing all names on cards.

BIRTHDAY CELEBRATIONS

These are becoming more popular today. The key to the door is now given much earlier. But many families still like the traditional twenty-first as a sign of true adulthood of their son or daughter. Many people now celebrate later birthday decades from thirty upwards. The general atmosphere is light-hearted and speeches should reflect this.

Checklist

- It is customary for the father or mother of the twenty-one-year-old to make the first speech. This should include a few well-chosen anecdotes about their daughter's or son's growing up, and should end by expressing delight at their coming of age.
- The main speech should be given by a close friend of the birthday person. This is usually more acceptable than the parental speech which often embarrasses the son or daughter with references to their childhood behaviour. Friends' speeches may include funny stories about their time at school or university, sporting achievements, holidays spent together.
- Humour is an essential ingredient for this type of speech. I recently attended a twenty-first birthday celebration where the speech was delivered in song, and also one for a fiftieth birthday celebration which was in the form of a funny poem.
- The speaker should wind up the proceedings by thanking the parents on behalf of the guests.
- The birthday person then should speak at rather more length, firstly thanking his or her parents, expressing

106

gratitude, and including others who have helped along the way. Often this occasion is attended by a number of the older members of the family, so the birthday person should mention them, with a few references to his or her own friends.

- If there is a sit-down dinner or buffet, speeches should be made after the dessert course is finished.

SAMPLE SPEECHES

Since this speech is usually made by the oldest friend of the married couple, it should be sincere. The speech can be adapted to suit various special anniversaries.

No. 1
Silver Wedding Party

Ladies and Gentlemen,
    My friends, I have been requested this evening to undertake a duty which I generally take great pains to avoid – that of giving a speech. I am not even going to try and get out of it on this occasion, because it is such an honour and pleasure to be asked to perform this duty. To be asked to propose the toast of the evening is a great privilege which nothing but a long and wonderful friendship could entitle me to claim. Today our host and hostess ––––– and ––––– are celebrating their twenty-five years of happy marriage. It is fitting that, on their Silver Wedding Day, we their friends should gather to drink their health and to wish them continued happiness.
    Time in his passing has dealt very gently with our two friends whose health I am about to propose; they reach their Silver Wedding Day with young hearts and faces as bright as silver itself, reflecting joy and happiness to all who know them.
    So, ladies and gentlemen, stand up for this glad celebration

of this Silver Wedding Day. The springtime of life may have gone, but the smiling summer remains. We look forward joyfully to a golden autumn when hopefully we shall join again to celebrate their harvest of good deeds and loving memories.

I will now ask you to drink with me, in hearty congratulations on this anniversary to ——— and ———, may health and happiness be with them now and in the future. May they have many happy returns of the day. God Bless them!

REPLY TO SILVER WEDDING TOAST BY THE HUSBAND

Ladies and Gentlemen,

You will, I am sure, pity me in the position in which I find myself. I am not, of course, referring to the matrimonial state, but to the position in which I have been placed by my good friend. He has praised highly, and so eloquently proposed my wife's health and my own.

Ladies and gentlemen, what can I say to thank you save that my wife and I do thank you from the bottom of our hearts? For myself, I must tell you that I do not deserve such lavish praise; but I may tell you that she, ———, does. It would take forever to express what she has been to me, what help and support in the battle of life she has given me by her love, encouragement and strength; and if I have been at all successful, it is to her that the greatest part of the credit is due.

Ladies and gentlemen, I thank you in the name of all my family. We are delighted to share this special day with you, and hope that there will be many more celebrations to share in the future.

We owe you another vote of thanks for your charming gifts – a kindly remembrance of our wedding day. For these, much thanks!

My wife, my children, and I appreciate your kind expressions, and reciprocate your good wishes. Ladies and gentlemen, once again we thank you!

No. 2
Silver Wedding

Ladies and Gentlemen,

I can almost say that I have looked forward to this moment for twenty-five years, for I was present at the wedding of the charming couple in whose honour I am speaking tonight. It is sometimes said that a friend who marries is a friend lost; but when ——— got married I not only retained his friendship, but gained another friend too. I have enjoyed the friendship of our charming hosts for nearly thirty years, and if we are still friends when their silver turns to gold, then I shall be very happy.

I can hardly believe my eyes tonight. Our host and hostess, ——— and ———, look much younger than their years; it is hard to believe that they have been married so long. Their obvious delight in each other is a joy to see. I think I can say that their honeymoon has lasted for twenty-five years, and looks like lasting for the rest of their lives.

Let us drink to their health, and wish them as much happiness in the future as they have had in the past. Ladies and gentlemen, to ——— and ———.

REPLY

Ladies and Gentlemen,

I have been looking forward to this opportunity of expressing the thanks of my wife and myself for your kind wishes and many charming gifts to mark this occasion in our married life.

Your good wishes are very much appreciated by us both. I can remember only one other occasion when I was almost lost for words. That occasion, of course, was our wedding day. All I could manage to stammer out then was that I thought I was the luckiest man in the whole universe. Ladies and gentlemen, twenty-five years later, I *know* that I am the luckiest man in the universe.

For twenty-five years I have shared my life with the perfect wife, while she has suffered a husband imperfect in all save

109

one thing: his love for her. Our mutual happiness has been brought to us by our lovely children, and many friends.

Tonight those friends are with us. And so we thank you all, not only for your kind wishes and presents, but for being our friends for so many years.

No. 3
Birthday Party
TOAST PROPOSED BY AN OLD FRIEND

Ladies and Gentlemen,

A very pleasant duty has devolved upon me today, and I only regret that I cannot do the subject more justice. I have been asked to propose to you the health of my good friend, ———, and to request that you drink the toast, wishing him many happy returns of the day. As one of his oldest friends I may be permitted to say a few words concerning him, and to express to those around me the great pleasure that association with him has given me and all with whom he has come in contact. Many of us have special reasons for knowing what a good fellow he is, and have experienced his kind hospitality and realise he is 'one of the best'. We recognise many present here who have grown up with our friendship, and it is a great and sure test of true friends when we see year after year the same smiling faces around us.

As a father/mother, husband/wife and friend ——— has won the esteem and admiration of all who have known him, and both in his public and private life he has set a high ideal before him. Ladies and gentlemen, I am sure you need no words of mine to convince you of our friend's fine qualities, nor will I longer detain you, but at once call upon you to join me in wishing ——— many happy returns of his birthday/80th birthday/etc.

REPLY TO BIRTHDAY TOAST
Always keep this reply brief, express surprise at all the good things said about you, and do not add to them.

Ladies and Gentlemen,

My old friend —— has almost left me speechless with the wonderful eulogy he has pronounced upon my unworthy self. But in one way he is right. I am deeply fortunate to have so many kind friends, and very glad to welcome you all. I am not so young as I was, and as we begin to descend the path of life we are brought face to face with many obstacles and rough steps which we had not even noticed before. But even so, nothing is so welcoming as the support of loyal/trusting/old/valued friends. Your friendship is a bright light upon the road.

To you, my friends, much of my happiness must be ascribed, and by your coming here today you have given me much joy. Thank you very much for your kind wishes and gifts, and I trust we may be spared to meet here for many a year to come.

No. 4
Birthday

Ladies and Gentlemen,

I have been asked to propose this toast because I am A —— B ——'s oldest friend. I am not sure if this does him justice. An old saying tells us that a man should be judged by his choice of friends, and I should hate to think that ——'s reputation was linked too closely to mine. I think I can say that it is only in this matter of choosing friends that I have better taste than he has.

I am not going to embarrass him by reciting a catalogue of his many fine qualities, but I think he will forgive me if I tell you of just one little experience that we shared many years ago. (Describe an incident to the credit of the subject of the toast.)

So, ladies and gentlemen, I ask you to join me in drinking the health of A —— B —— and in wishing him many happy returns of his birthday. May he have many more birthdays to come!

111

REPLY

Ladies and Gentlemen,

C———— D———— has done me many acts of friendship in the past. Today, he has credited me with virtues I do not possess, and has discreetly omitted to mention my many failings. I am not going to correct him, because if I did you would start doubting that ———— is as fine a man as you know him to be. The fact is, I am exceedingly fortunate to have so many good friends, and the proof of my good fortune is in the company that has honoured me by being here today. There is an old saying, 'Be sure your friends will find you out.' I don't believe it, for my friends have never found me out, and I hope they never do. Ladies and gentlemen, thank you very much for your kind wishes.

No. 5
Coming of Age
(WOMAN)

Ladies and Gentlemen,

My task tonight is an honour rather than a duty, for I am sure that I am generally envied for being chosen to propose the health of ———— on her twenty-first birthday.

My only qualification is that I have had the pleasure of wishing her many happy returns on all/most of her other birthdays.

It seems like only yesterday when I had the privilege of sharing her first birthday party. You will, I am sure, appreciate that I look back on those days rather wistfully, for I am unlikely to get any further opportunities of this nature.

I have watched ———— grow up from a pretty child to a lovely woman; her cheerful enthusiasm broaden into charm. To me she has always been sweet and lovable, and I am sure she will remain the same for the rest of her life. Ladies and gentlemen, I ask you to join me in drinking the health of ———— and wishing her many happy returns on her twenty-first birthday.

112

REPLY
A few words of thanks is all that is required here.

Ladies and Gentlemen,
Please don't ask me for a speech. I wouldn't know where to begin. Thank you from the bottom of my heart, thank you!

Quotations

AGE

The Grecian ladies counted their age from their marriage, not their birth.

Homer

The young have aspirations that never come to pass, the old have reminiscences of what never happened.

Saki

Men are like wine. Some turn to vinegar, but the best improve with age.

C.E. Joad

If beauty is a letter of introduction – wrinkles are a good résumé.

Mary Ellen Pickham

A woman is as young as her knees.

Mary Quant

I was born in 1962, true. And the room next to me was 1963.

Joan Rivers

Christenings

It is customary to propose a toast to the health of the new baby on these occasions. This is usually done by the baby's godfather, or an old friend of the parents. It should be light-hearted, and include a compliment to the mother and father. If the godfather is a grandfather, he can recall an anecdote about the mother or father as a baby.

No. 1
Toast to the Health of the Baby

It is a pity that our special guest cannot, as yet, say a few words himself. For if he could, I am sure that this fine young baby/fellow/boy/girl would say how pleased he is to be here with us. I am sure he would also say how delighted he was to be born to such wonderful parents, ——— and ———, of whose friendship, we in turn, are particularly proud.

His good upbringing, care and love are most certainly assured, and it is with great pleasure that I offer all our good wishes for him today. May his young life blossom under their love, and may he live long to be a source of joy and happiness to them.

Raise your glasses, ladies and gentlemen, and drink to the health, happiness and long fulfilled life of ———. God Bless him.

REPLY BY THE FATHER

Ladies and Gentlemen,

I thank my old friend for so kindly proposing the health of our little child, ———, and to welcome him upon his first stage in life.

My wife and I accept and greatly appreciate all your good

114

wishes. Many very handsome and flattering things have been said of my wife and myself which we do not deserve. But there is at any rate one point upon which I can speak, and that is the pleasure it has given us to welcome you all here today for this happy occasion. We are greatly obliged to all our friends for your presence, and presents, your company and your good wishes.

Before I sit down, I would ask you to drink to the godmother and the godfathers, here today. Their healths and their families – may they all live long and prosper!

No. 2
Christening

Ladies and Gentlemen,

I have the great pleasure in proposing the health of our robust-looking/sounding guest of honour. This is his first real public appearance, and I am sure you will agree he has made a great success out of it. It is perhaps a little early to discuss his character, but already he has turned out to be a little charmer. Of course he ought to be a fine boy/girl, because he has such wonderful parents. We know that ——— and ——— will give him all the love and care needed to make his childhood happy and secure; and I am sure that he in turn will bring great joy to them.

So I ask you to drink to the health of A ——— B ——— (baby's names), and may he have a long and happy life.

REPLY BY THE FATHER

Ladies and Gentlemen,

I must apologise on behalf of my son, who regrets that he is unable to reply to your toast himself, and has asked me to do the job for him. I must say that this is not the worst job I have had to do for him in his short life, and I do not doubt that there are more difficult jobs ahead.

My wife and I are grateful to you all for the flattering things you have said about us, which we do not deserve. We are very ordinary parents, but I hope you will pardon me if I point out that this is no ordinary baby.

We want to thank you for coming to give A ——— B ——— (name) your support on this important occasion in his life, and our special thanks are due to those who have kindly acted as his sponsors. May I ask you to drink to their health too?

Ladies and gentlemen, to the baby's godmother and god-fathers!

Quotations

CHILDREN

Before I got married I had six theories about bringing up children; now I have six children, and no theories.

Earl of Rochester

A loud noise at one end and no sense of responsibility at the other.

Father Ronald Knox

Don't take up a man's time talking about the smartness of your children; he wants to talk to you about the smartness of his.

Ed Howe

Every baby born into the world is a finer one than the last.

Charles Dickens

To bring up a child in the way he should go, travel that way yourself once in a while.

Josh Billings

He followed in his father's footsteps, but his gait was somewhat erratic.

Nicolas Bentley

After-dinner Speaking

If you don't strike oil in five minutes STOP BORING.

American Toastmaster

GENERAL ADVICE

The after-dinner speech should be considered in a different way to any other kind of speech. The after-dinner occasion is part of a social entertainment, the accent being on pleasure. It is accompanied by eating and drinking.

Unfortunately many otherwise delightful occasions are spoiled by the speech-making, which usually takes place after the meal. Just as one is mellowing under the influence of good food and drink, the speech-making begins. The speakers have a captive audience, and all too often take advantage of this fact.

Many after-dinner speeches are badly prepared and last too long. No matter how excellent the speaker, an after-dinner speech should be kept to a minimum, and never long. It should be light and witty, and match the food, i.e. digestible.

Very often speakers feel that their performance should be no less than brilliant. This is a mistake, as few of us can produce Churchillian masterpieces. Instead aim to put yourself in the shoes of the audience. If you were sitting out there, what would you like to hear? The answer would probably include the words 'brief' and 'entertaining'.

Steps for Planning the After-dinner Speech

- Prepare with great care an interesting *introduction* or

117

beginning, keeping in mind the audience and the general theme of your speech.

- Before getting into detail, think of the *ending*. Are you going to end with a witty anecdote, or a quotation? Many potentially good speeches fall down because the speaker has not thought about the ending. Remember you want to end on a 'high', to go out with a bang. Many speakers are panicked into an ending that lacks punch or even relevance.
- What goes into the *body* or the middle of the speech is like a sandwich-filling, that depends upon so many considerations that it is impossible to do more than offer general advice. This type of speech is very personal, and is dependent upon the speaker's personality, the type of audience and their mood at the moment of speaking, and lastly, the speaker's ability.
- Wit, when used, should arise in a spontaneous and natural way. It should never be laboured or lengthy. Advantage may be taken of something said by another speaker. This should always be done in the spirit of good clean fun.

Speaking of fun reminds me of the story told by a parish clergyman who had returned home to England after spending most of his life in an African mission. The occasion was a simple one – a Harvest Thanksgiving social and supper. The audience comprised his parishioners, their family and friends. The little man stood quietly for something under five minutes while fun simply flowed out of him. He said nothing that was brilliant or intellectual and afterwards it was difficult to recall any particularly memorable phrase he had said. Nonetheless, when he sat down, the audience laughed loudly and unashamedly and felt the better for it.

He told of an elderly priest whose long celibacy had made him old-maidishly fussy about trifles and who had a particular liking for buttered toast – perhaps because it was so essentially English. But the toast had to be crisp; he could not endure it soggy and the Mission cook could never seem to produce it any other way. The priest read the cook a great lecture one day on the art of making toast English style, and ended up with the statement that pieces of toast should never be laid upon each other when made as this led to sogginess. They must be kept upright and separate, he said. For several weeks after this the toast came to the table as crisp as the heart of man could desire and the old priest was delighted. Wishing to express his appreciation he paid a special visit to the kitchen and found the cook making more toast while holding the pieces already made upright and separate between the toes of his left foot!

Although not a hilariously funny story – indeed, the sensitive may find it slightly nauseating – the audience roared at it. Which only goes to prove that it is not so much *what* is said as *how* it is said that counts.

The secret of this speaker's success was the fun he created. His story was based upon genuine experience, was kindly and sympathetic, and never patronising.

It is often difficult to advise what should follow the initial ice-breaker in the after-dinner speech. What you say will depend very much on circumstances at the time, and the common bond that binds the listeners (rugby-players, golfers, lawyers, philatelists etc.). It will also depend on the content of the speeches which have preceded yours.

You should however prepare a speech on broad lines, but for the above reasons you may have to alter, extend or reduce this as you go.

THE HOBBY-HORSE

Riding one's hobby-horse should be avoided by all public speakers. Most of us have a hobby-horse and will ride it if given some small encouragement – or even not! It is a breach of good manners to include this in the after-dinner speech.

RESEARCH

The most difficult things for a man to do are to climb a wall leaning towards you, to kiss a girl leaning away from you, and to make an after-dinner speech.

Winston Churchill

119

Research is an important element in getting the after-dinner speech right, as well as all the general preparation, i.e. knowing how long you will speak, the administration details, the audience profile etc.

The following information will help with your planning:

- Background history of the organisation/club/company, when it was founded and how many members it has.
- Names of the club officers/directors/chairman.
- Is it part of a world-wide movement, e.g. Rotary, Amnesty International, to which some tribute or acknowledgement should be paid?

The Speech Should Include:

- Thanks to your hosts.
- An appropriate quote about the organisation, its history, etc. Or, if you have been asked to speak about your own industry or company, start by telling the audience something personal about yourself, for example, that you enjoy golf/cricket/ sailing/eating out/collecting antiques/first editions.

Audiences enjoy hearing something personal about the speaker: it helps to humanise you. This audience is neutral and not necessarily friendly and supportive as at a wedding or christening.

Next, say something about the industry and your company. Include some facts and figures, but keep this to a minimum; perhaps give export earnings, jobs created etc.

After-dinner speaking is perhaps one of the most enjoyable of all speaking engagements. A captive audience, well wined and dined, should be a speaker's joy. However important the occasion or distinguished the audience, they do not want to hear a dry lecture or boring monologue. They want to be entertained.

The speech itself requires the same preparation as any other. It needs a flow of ideas as well as words. And the more the words are laced with wit, the more likely that their wisdom will hit home.

- Keep this speech brief.
- Lace it with humour.

As you approach the end – remember what it is you have been called to do. For example, if responding to a toast:

- Start by thanking the person who proposed it.
- Repeat your delight at having been asked to speak and your good wishes to the organisation who invited you.

For more than eighty years the Guild of Professional Toastmasters has recorded each year the names of the worst after-dinner speakers endured by its members. No bribery will make the Guild reveal the poor speakers, but here are a few words of advice from those acknowledged to be among the very best.

As to advice for would-be orators, I would say that, in order to take them by surprise – and surprise is an essential ingredient in good speaking, as it is in military strategy and in love – it is imperative to take risks, by taking yourself by surprise. Don't rehearse too meticulously. Don't learn things by heart.

Sir Peter Ustinov

Prepare, pretend to be confident, and always flatter the audience. Don't fall over, pick your nose, or pontificate.

Tony Ball

Use humour, use notes, and use your hands. Smile, weave stories around the appropriate 'characters' present, and exude a friendly sincerity. Be natural, be topical and only drink during toasts. Emphasise in threes, include a brief serious message – and pray.

Tony Ball

AFTER-DINNER SPEAKING

Be yourself. Know your subject. Talk – don't read. Humour must be related to the topic. Avoid phrases like 'I shall have more to say about this later.' 'Finally' means I am ending this speech *now*.

Baroness Phillips

The ability to tell stories is a plus for the after-dinner speaker. The true raconteur 'sees' the story in his mind as he tells it. While a story may be fiction, it is, in the telling, a passing fact in the mind. If you use the radio technique it should allow audiences to listen in that way, the words allowing them to form their own mind pictures of the plot development. If you have not thought of story-telling on these lines before, then try to think of your anecdotes in the present tense as *about* to happen. This gives them more impact than quoting from past history.

If using true anecdotes take care. The trouble with updating a true anecdote is that someone in the audience may know the true story. A veteran after-dinner speaker tells of the time he heard a young speaker telling an anecdote about Yorkshire cricket to be interrupted by an irate veteran who bawled: 'That was not Freddie Trueman, it was Abe Waddington – before you were born, lad!'

The room went quiet and the speaker stumbled on awkwardly.

AFTER-DINNER HUMOUR

LAUGHTER IS INFECTIOUS
Have you ever sat near someone in the theatre who has a loud, hearty laugh? If the show is not particularly funny, or it doesn't seem so to you anyway, this laugh is irritating at first. But after a little while you find yourself laughing too. The laughing has become infectious, and you laugh in spite of yourself. The message is that the whole success of the after-dinner speaker is dependent upon passing on to the audience your sense of the enjoyment of the occasion.

With the emphasis on enjoyment, humour is a serious

business. On other occasions, if the audience is not comfortable with your jokes, they may say so. It is more likely they will cough or shuffle uncomfortably in their seats. At an after-dinner event, courtesy dictates that the audience sit through the speech without comment, that they smile and clap at the end.

JOKES

Jokes are also popular on these occasions. The double entendre, the risqué, in their proper place can be entertaining, but for most occasions I would advise against them. These tend to crop up a lot at sports dinners. Some years ago, a matronly lady mayoress tried to inject some humour into her speech. She told her good citizens a story, roughly as follows:

> Two RAF pilots during the war took two girls in secret on a flight over enemy territory. They were shot up and with the machine in flames one officer said to the other: 'There's only two parachutes. What do we do with the girls?'
> 'F———— 'em.'
> 'Have we got time?'

Quite naturally the parochial audience were shocked, and took exception to the lady's idea of an after-dinner joke. The joke was probably not relevent to her theme, but if her subject had been war, then here is a more acceptable alternative.

> Two Land Army girls had a night on the town and crept back into their hostel in the small hours. They had to climb barbed wire, scale a wall and roof to get back into their quarters undetected. As they lowered themselves down a pipe one said 'I feel like a commando'.
> The other replied 'So do I – but where are we going to find any this time of night?'

More or less the same story, but one which is not likely to cause offence.

It is said that there is no such thing as a new joke; they have all been told before. This may be true, but old jokes can be approached in a different way and revamped to take on a new look. All that has been said about humour applies here, with the emphasis on brevity.

A golfing story that may illustrate the point about brevity concerns a four-ball match:

The first player swung badly and said: 'Lord! what a slice!'

The second followed suit and snarled: 'What a ghastly hook!'

The third player took a tremendous swipe and roared: 'Topped the ****** again!'

The fourth man swung violently three times without touching the ball at all, smiled gently and said: 'Tough course!'

THE DIALECT JOKE

At a dinner given by the Irish Anglers' Association an Irishman, proposing a toast to 'The Visitors', told what was an otherwise good story about a Scotsman, in an excruciating imitation of a Glasgow accent. An Englishman told a story about an Englishman, a Scotsman and an Irishman. His cockney accent was superb, but the other two accents were even worse than the first speaker.

If you can tell a dialect story well, it is a popular style of humour; but if it is not accurate it will fall flat. Every national speech has its own distinctive pronunciations and rhythm. The success of dialect lies in its inflections, and unless these are right the rest of the imitation will not compensate. Unless you are confident you can carry this off well, leave the dialect jokes out of your speech.

STANCE

We have said in previous chapters that the speaker should stand confidently with his hands hanging loosely and unselfconsciously by his side. If he is using a flipchart or showing slides, then it is appropriate to hold a pen, remote control, or even notes, as long as they don't become a distraction for the audience.

At a dinner, however, *one* hand lightly in the pocket is permissible, and gives just that touch of informality that the occasion warrants. *Both* hands in the pockets is always wrong; it is slovenly and can look positively rude and objectionable.

The other rules are the same as before: head up looking out to the audience. Owing to the positioning of tables, it is sometimes difficult to maintain eye contact with everyone. Yve Newbold, a successful businesswoman and experienced public speaker gives some excellent advice on this subject:

> I try to look at the audience in a sweep that is like my Flymo doing the lawn, a sort of left to right and back again arc, starting at the front and working on down the audience.

You will stand and look as you feel. The speaker who shrinks mentally shrinks physically. Think well of yourself and you will carry it off well, you will also look good.

Head up – Relaxed body – Pleasant appearance – Positive attitude.

FULL AFTER-DINNER SPEECH SAMPLE

The following is an after-dinner speech which I believe combines many positive aspects. For the speaker who is new to after-dinner speaking it provides a useful blueprint, and combines the many key elements present in all successful speeches and toasts. My thanks to Edward Stanners for his kind permission to reproduce it here.

Brief:	To give a talk at a dinner for the Worshipful Company of Dyers and Finishers.
Objective:	To say thank you on behalf of the guests.
Time:	Fifteen minutes.
Audience:	Members of the Company of the Dyers and Finishers and their guests (350 in all).

Prime Warden, Renter Warden, My Lord, Gentlemen,

When Prime Warden approached me some months ago to see if I could condense my recent work 'The Merits of Dyeing Cellulosic Fibres with Mordant Dyestuffs' into a two-hour speech for you tonight, I was at once flattered and dismayed . . . flattered because I have spent the last twenty-five years involved in dyeing in one way or another . . . dismayed because I knew next to nothing of the subject.

You see, Gentlemen, I am a charlatan . . . for decades I have lived with the guilty secret that throughout my three years' studies, Dyeing and Finishing was on a Tuesday. And to my shame Tuesday was the standard day off for au pair girls. I could easily talk to you about the best way of opening a conversation with a Parisienne . . . I could amuse you with anecdotes of pretty fräuleins . . . but dyestuffs are not my strong point.

That said, I have a lifetime dealing with what someone once correctly described as a delicate mixture of science and black magic. I hope that in the next few minutes I can impart some of the flavour of the Industry.

A little over quarter of a century ago during a six-month stay in the Outer Hebrides, I spent an afternoon with the last person still to be dyeing Harris Tweed yarns – or rather the raw wool from which they are spun – in cauldrons using mosses etc. for colouring. Twenty-five years later I worked with machines which can see colour and can provide a recipe for a given shade taking into account the stock of dye available and the resultant costs . . . I have seen technology almost totally take over. In twenty-five years we have gone from dyeing a few pounds of wool in a cauldron to dyeing a ton and more in vessels the size of a bus.

Along the way many names have fallen prey to the times – great mills have closed or almost done so.

My first exposure to textiles came when as a sixteen-year-old I had a summer holiday job working as the groundsman assistant of a giant mill called Salts of Saltaire. Built in 1853 the mill and its surrounding village provide a livelihood, schooling, worship, hospital etc. to the 4000 operatives and their families.

Part of the responsibilities involved marking the football and rugby pitches. For those of you who don't know, these are marked by filling a three-wheeled tank with a mixture of marker and strong weedkiller and driving the front wheel down a string stretched tightly between the flagpoles to create a straight line.

Ever one in those days for a short cut I decided that the process did not need to be so laborious and that provided that one keep an eye on the far corner flag, a straight line had to result . . . Setting off in gay abandon . . . and in those days gay abandon had a different meaning . . . it was not until the three-quarter point that I felt it necessary to look back over my handiwork . . . Imagine my horror when I saw a line which strayed fully three feet either side of true. I have often wondered since how many matches were won or lost on my carelessness.

Fifteen years later I was to return to that mill, determined to be much more careful, as its Managing Director.

This, my first heavy responsibility, was to be a daunting experience. A few days before I actually started I learnt of losses of £70,000 per month, and realised that we were in for a long hard battle, since many of the losses stemmed from poor relations with shop floor and management.

Now at this point I should perhaps explain that in the North certainly at that time, there was a gap between the different strata of society which could be cut with a knife. It was only a few weeks earlier that I had moved house and been forcibly reminded of the gulf when the removal men carried in a long backless sofa with a raised end and asked where we wanted the Chasse Lounge. When an hour later the carpet fitter, heading for the bathroom which connected with a bedroom, announced that he was just going to tackle the En Suet, I realised that perhaps those Tuesdays spent with French au pair girls weren't pure hedonism . . .

So, full of a mixture of trepidation and enthusiasm I threw myself into the first day at the Mill, proud to be its Managing

Director. By seven o'clock I was tired but happy. I felt the mistrust between the operative and Director could be bridged . . . I felt that together we could get it right.

But I decided to put my newfound confidence into practice and set off to talk to the evening shift. I soon encountered two older ladies – menders, that most skilled of occupations as they sew in missing yarns exactly copying the complex weave and tension – and walked up to them. 'Good Evening ladies, I'm Edward Stanners.' Stony silence. 'I'm the new Managing Director.' Worse stony silence. By now panic was setting in. Could I have gone wrong? Did they want me to bridge the gap? After what seemed like a minute one of them put her face closer to mine, looking at me as if I was a Martian. 'Ee love,' she said, 'you're a bit young aren't you?'

I shrugged this off by saying that I had a lot of experience and felt we could crack it if we worked together. The battle was not yet over . . . the other lady came closer. 'Ey love, I've worked 'ere 19 years and I've never talked to an 'igh up.' 'Ay, and I've done 21 years and I've never met an 'igh up.' I learnt in one five-minute conversation that the Directors had been so elevated they were unaware of the basic problems of the business. Months later when I returned to the same section and the ladies were picking out of a batch of cloth the seed contamination which comes in some Australian wools and I asked if we were winning, I realised that we were when one of the ladies said 'Love, it's like picking fly shit out of black pepper . . . but we'll do it'. Difficult but humorous times . . .

Talking of humorous occasions I should, out of deference to this evening, try to shed a little light on what my fellow guests can expect from the remainder of this very pleasant evening.

Fellow guests, I have an advantage over some of you since I attended a daytime function as a guest of the Company earlier in the year. Without revealing too many of the Company's secrets, I can tell you that the event began badly when our transport was held up waiting for the Senior Officer whose coat had been caught in the lift gates of an underground station. Since that day was an aperitif to this evening, I began to wonder whether fate may not be a little too unkind to the Company for comfort . . .

I should have known better . . . Once the raincoat incident was behind us we never looked back. Indeed the day's events are best summarised by a comment I overhead when a host asked a guest if he was comfortably seated, only to have a nearby wag say 'Comfortable . . . he's as comfortable as a newt.' Come to think of it, some of my fellow guests are looking very *comfortable*, Prime Warden . . .

One of the things I did learn during my previous day as your guest was a little of the history of the Companies in general and this one in particular. Again, at the risk of boring those of you who know much about the history, I wonder if I might tell my fellow guests some of the background which some wag described as 'A bit like radar . . . you know it works but you don't know quite how.'

Livery Companies representing almost every facet of medieval industry – and frequently different factions of an industry – were established in the main through the fourteenth, fifteenth and sixteenth centuries. Originally Companies took over the houses of noblemen since these offered ready-built banqueting halls. Accounts vary as to why they needed to be established but it appears most likely that at a time when the Free Market Economy was at its height, both the patrons, particularly Royalty, and the artisans themselves, realised that both had something to gain by forming an exclusive body. Since much of the early revenue for the Companies came from their letting out their halls, I suppose they were a cross between the Village Hall and the CBI.

While I found scant reference to individual Companies I did discover facts about trade which deserve a wider audience.

It came as no surprise to find that in Roman times Weavers were always slaves and controlling them became so difficult that they were ultimately branded to make identification easier. Dyers appear not to have been so

129

branded but when one bears in mind that one of the most common dyes was a mixture of oak beetles ground up in a man's urine, they would appear to have had quite enough of a cross to bear.

Going forward, in an account of 1549 Textile Workers were already seen as a lazy bunch 'working a little in summer though they be half idle the residue of the year.'

Those of you in the textile trade will know that today there is an increasing fear of power being concentrated in few hands. *Plus* infinite *change*, gentlemen. In 1610 a report on weaving read 'The Fellowship was spring full of monopolies engrossing the grand staple commodities of cloth into so few men's hands.'

On the face of it though this was not a bad thing. In the fifteenth century, 80% of Britain's total exports were cloth, 90% passing through London. Your company has a wonderful history, Prime Warden.

Gentlemen, I was disappointed to find only a few medieval anecdotes. However, being here to sing for my supper I did find one story which seems perfect to round off my part in tonight's proceedings. It is taken from an unnamed Guild's records of 1431 . . . 'On July 1st was the first feast made in our fair hall at which feast was the Mayor and many a worshipful person more, beside the whole craft at which feast was drunken two pipes of wine and nine barrels of ale and all the appurtences that longeth hereto'.

Prime Warden, Officers of the Company, your guests have enjoyed many pipes of wine and the appurtences that longeth plenty. We are feeling more comfortable by the minute. I thank you for your hospitality. Such a sumptuous event more than compensates for the odd problem in my textile career to date.

I and my fellow guests have been honoured to attend an element of our nation's history. At the risk of being jingoistic, this evening's pageant is part of what made Britain great. Thank you Prime Warden for your kindness tonight. We look forward to becoming more comfortable as the hour gets later. THANK YOU.

FEEDBACK

When asked if he had received any feedback on his performance, Mr Stanners said it was 'Positive and congratulatory',
even though he believed that this was not one of his best
speeches.

Note: Only the very best of speakers believe that 'the best is
yet to come'.

SUMMARY

This is a good point to reflect on the advice given earlier in
the book. Much has been made of the importance of areas
such as structure, putting the script together, and putting the
message across. Having read about the dos and don'ts of
preparation and delivery, you now want to see how it works
in practice.

No matter how good a speech, it can always be improved.
A perfect speech is not possible for mere humans. There are,
however, some excellent speakers who give very creditable
performances. Part of what I do for a living involves individual training for speakers who wish to have an objective
assessment of their performance. They attend a training
session for many reasons. For example, they may never have
made a speech before, and perhaps don't know where to
start. Or they have a specific speaking engagement and need
some assistance and feedback on performance. Often very
experienced speakers will come along, mainly for reassur-
ance that they are good! Like one Chief Executive who
believed he rated 7 or 8 in a scale of 10 for speaking ability
(his objective was to become a 10). He was indeed a very
accomplished speaker, but nonetheless he left the session
with one or two hints to improve his performance. The
purpose of telling you this is that no matter how good a
speaker you are, there is always room for improvement. With
this in mind, resolve to improve your speech-making.

● Start a Resource File *now*.

When you hear an interesting story or statistic from the media jot it down, you never know when it will be useful. For example as I am typing this section, the media is reporting statistics on crime. 'A survey has shown that staff account for 50% of shop theft.'

- *The Times*, *Observer*, *Telegraph* and *Guardian* newspapers all have interesting sections such as 'Sayings of the Week', 'Backbites,' 'That was the Week', 'On This Day'. These include historical events, quotations and anecdotes – always useful for speeches.

- Learn from your mistakes.
  Every speaker makes mistakes at some time or other. When you have delivered a speech which hasn't quite gone as well as you had hoped, don't dwell on the negative, you have probably included many positive elements. Shortly after you make the speech (within a few days), examine where you went wrong. Did you allow sufficient time for preparation? Have a structure? Mis-read the audience? Once you have identified the problem you can then resolve to put it right next time.

- Learn from other speakers, particularly the good ones.
  We can learn a lot by watching how others approach a subject or audience; how they cope when courage deserts them, or when things go wrong.

There is a very good story told of the late comedian, Tony Hancock. Hancock was renowned for his dislike of making speeches and memorising scripts, not to mention the stress involved. However, he was persuaded to attend a charity function at the Savoy Hotel. The speech ahead of Hancock was going well, and given by an elderly Catholic priest. By all accounts, the speech was wonderful, delivered with wit and enthusiasm. The audience gave him a standing ovation. When the priest sat down, Tony's face was like granite.

Then he was introduced, and stood up, applauded by a receptive and expectant sea of faces. Tony's notes were in his fist. He waved them airily, nodded around the room and spoke.

AFTER-DINNER SPEAKING

Just before we came in for dinner, Father and I met in the gents and you all know now what a lad he is for a joke, my goodness me, yes. He said to me, 'Wouldn't it be funny if we exchanged speeches and I did yours and you did mine?' So we did, and you've just heard mine. This is his and I'm not doing this load of rubbish – good evening!

Presentation
of Awards

I'm not interested in an inanimate statue of a little bald
man. I like something with long blonde curls.

Woody Allen

GENERAL ADVICE

Awards have been in existence for a long time. Everyone has at
one time or another in their lives attended an award-giving
ceremony, even if it was only the end-of-year speech night at
school. There are many award night occasions, but whatever
the occasion may be, the general guidelines for preparing and
giving a good speech apply to any occasion, although award-
giving functions have tended to create their own protocol.

It is even more important on this occasion to try and inject
some of your own personality into the speech. Remember the
audience has heard it all before. If you stick by the formula
below for making presentation speeches you should have no
problems on the big day or night.

The purpose of the presentation speech is to honour the
recipient and praise him for his accomplishments before handing over the award.

RECEIVING AN AWARD – THE FOUR KEY POINTS

- Express your appreciation of the award and acknowledge the
  honour.
- Thank the presenter.

- Give a quick thanks to family, friends, your company.
- Finish up by expressing what the award means to you and say something about how it will spur you on to even greater things.

THE SCHOOL

SPEECH DAY

In the past, most guest speakers at school speech days played a role in public life, e.g. politicians or mayor. But there is an increasing tendency to bring in speakers from other areas, such as a leading light in the sporting community, a former student, or school governor. Sometimes the guest speaker hands out the prizes as well, and the guest should do some research to link the school with his subject. For example the sporting guest could refer to any former pupil who has gained distinction in the sporting field.

The speaker must remember that a large part of his audience on school speech-making occasions will be boys and girls, and he should adapt his speech accordingly. Don't 'talk down' to them.

SAMPLE SPEECHES

No. 1
Presentation of Prizes
(SPORTS DAY)

Ladies and Gentlemen,

Before I present the prizes, I am expected to make a speech. You probably think that is hard on you, but I assure you that it is much harder on me. So for my sake as well as yours, it is going to be short.

I have been greatly impressed with what I have seen here today. And when I say impressed, I am not only referring to the time-keeper's records, although these reveal some pretty fine achievements. But the really fine thing was the enthusiasm shown by the competitors – not only those who won prizes, but by all of you.

The victors have achieved great things here today, so our first congratulations go to them. They have every right to feel proud of their achievements. But we must also congratulate the losers. Not because they lost – but because they did their best. They strove hard to win. They put in all their efforts; and what fine, courageous efforts they were!

So congratulations to you all – but especially to the winners. (Follow with the presentation of the prizes.)

A Vote of Thanks is given after presentations, and also after other school occasions such as a play or concert. This should be brief, a few words of thanks (often followed by a rousing three cheers!)

No. 2
The School
This toast is usually proposed by an Old Boy, and it should be brief and simple.

Gentlemen,

The Old School Tie has been the subject of so many music-hall jokes that one might expect it to have been laughed out of existence. Yet there seems to be plenty of evidence to the contrary here tonight; and the fact that it has survived so much ridicule surely proves that it is by no means a meaningless symbol.

Most loyalties are difficult to explain, and loyalty to the School is no exception. Old Boys' Associations differ from other societies in one important respect: their members are not proposed and elected, and indeed have little say in the matter of qualification for membership. The only thing that we have in common, on the face of it, is that our respective parents happened to send us to the same educational establishment; and one might ask what bond can exist among us. The answer is not far away. As boys we were drawn together in friendship towards a common ideal. Honour, teamwork and comradeship. These enduring qualities are the true Spirit of the School. Gentlemen – The School!

Quotations

EDUCATION

A child miseducated is a child lost.

John F. Kennedy

Education: A debt due from present to future generations.

George Peabody

'Whom are you?' said he, for he had been to night school.

George Ade

The advantage of a classical education is that it enables you to despise the wealth which it prevents you from achieving.

Russell Green

A school should not be a preparation for life. A school should be life.

Elbert Hubbard

Education is helping the child realise his potentialities.

Erich Fromm

The education of man is never completed until he dies.

Robert E. Lee

I've over-educated myself in all the things I shouldn't have known at all.

Noel Coward

Political and Business

Kissing babies gives me asthma.

John F. Kennedy

POLITICAL

If you are asked to introduce a candidate then it is important that you do your homework. You are not expected to go into details of his policy, but the way that you approach the introduction will have some bearing on setting the general mood of the audience. When speaking about politics on any occasion, you will find that some of your audience will be hostile.

Bear this in mind, and keep your introductions short and to the point.

Introducing the Candidate at an Election Meeting

Ladies and Gentlemen,

As chairman of this meeting I have the pleasure of introducing Mr ———, to represent the interests of ——— in Parliament. As you know he is the representative of the ——— Party, and as you will have guessed, I, too, am a supporter of that Party. I believe in its principles and its policy, and I am convinced that if it is returned to power in this Election – as I am sure it will be – every member of the community will benefit.

Mr ——— is, in my opinion, admirably suited to represent this Borough, not only because his politics are sound, but he is a man of great integrity, ability and vision.

I introduce him to you, ladies and gentlemen, and I trust you will give him the good hearing he deserves.

138

POLITICAL AND BUSINESS

A Municipal candidate should be introduced by the Chairman, and this short introduction can be more focused, mentioning local affairs, and including any environmental/educational/employment issues etc. Particular mention should be given to the topical issue on which the candidate is taking a strong line, e.g. crime.

Toast – Our Member of Parliament
This toast may be proposed at a Party gathering or at a more general function. The wording should be acceptable to everyone, and therefore not be controversial or political. This is generally a very short toast, complimenting the MP on his work and pledging continued support.

Ladies and Gentlemen,
It is with great pleasure that I rise to propose the toast of our Member of Parliament. You will be relieved to hear that I am not going to make a speech. I am sure that after the last eventful session at Westminster, Mr ——— will have heard enough of speech-making. Our MP may be surprised to know how closely we read his speeches, and we know that he has never forgotten the interests of his constituents. Since he was elected in ——— he has worked tirelessly to serve the interests of his constituents. His presence with us today is one more example of his concern for local affairs. He can rest assured that his efforts are recognised and appreciated by all in the community.
Ladies and Gentlemen, I give you the toast of Mr ———, our MP.

Quotations

POLITICS

Never lose your temper with the press or the public is the major rule of political life.

Christabel Pankhurst

POLITICAL AND BUSINESS

The First Lady is an unpaid public servant elected by one person – her husband.

Lady Bird Johnson

In politics, if you want anything said, ask a man; if you want anything done, ask a woman.

Margaret Thatcher

Politicians are the same all over. They promise to build a bridge even when there's no river.

Nikita Khrushchev

Every country has the government it deserves.

Joseph De Maistre

We all know that Prime Ministers are wedded to the truth, but like other wedded couples they sometimes live apart.

(H.H. Munro)

An honest politician is one who, when he is bought, will stay bought.

Simon Cameron (Republican politician)

He thinks like a Tory and talks like a radical, and that's so important nowadays.

Oscar Wilde

BUSINESS

Presentation to Employee Getting Married

Ladies and Gentlemen,

I have two pleasant tasks to perform today. One is to offer to ———, our congratulations and best wishes on the occasion of his marriage; the other is to present him with a small gift from the staff. Tomorrow ——— will go off on his honeymoon and when we see him again he will be a different man. I have not had the pleasure of meeting the bride, but I am sure that ——— has made a splendid choice, he always had good taste.

We wish them every happiness, and offer our very best wishes to ——— and the future ———.

Presentation on the Occasion of a Retiring Employee

Mr Chairman, Colleagues and Friends,
It will seem strange to walk through the factory/Accounts/Personnel department without seeing ———. In the past ——— months/years, he has established himself as an example of all that is best in our industry/organisation.

Everyone here today is united in our praise for ———. Let me list some of his achievements during the past ——— months/years.

1.
2.
3.

Our friend and colleague ———, has been an example to us all, we shall miss him.

We thank him and we wish him well.

Sporting Toasts

Always play fair, and think fair; and if you win don't crow
about it; and if you lose don't fret.

Eden Philpotts

GENERAL ADVICE

The convention for sporting toasts is that the toast be proposed
by the captain of the winning team and answered by his
opposite number. Sometimes the toast is proposed by the
captain of the home team, irrespective of the result of the
match.

If your side has won – then don't make a meal of it, play
success down and mention how difficult it was for your team to
win. If you have lost – don't make excuses, admit that the better
team won the day. You could also add that you will seek
revenge next time.

Sometimes both teams are toasted together, particularly
when there has been a big margin of victory.

SAMPLE SPEECHES

The following toasts can be adapted to suit any other team
sport.

No. 1
Our Opponents (Cricket)

Gentlemen,
I have the greatest pleasure in proposing to you the toast
of our opponents. I know you will agree with me that we

had an excellent game. We are fortunate that we just managed to scrape a win, and on paper it may look a comfortable victory. In fact our opponents gave us more than a few uncomfortable moments. Of course I am pleased we won, but even more delighted that we had such a terrific game. Our opponents were not only accomplished sportsmen, but they certainly showed us a thing or two about fielding.

It is not the result we shall remember of this game so much as the spirit in which it was played. The next time we meet we shall try to win again – although I must admit we know that we have a tough task ahead. But whatever the result, we know that we shall have a good game, played in the spirit in which cricket should always be played.

Gentlemen, I give you the toast of our opponents, the ——, A —— B ——, (give the name of the club, followed by the name of their captain.)

REPLY TO THE TOAST OF OUR OPPONENTS

Gentlemen,

On behalf of a very chastened team, I wish to thank you for your most cordial toast. We have been soundly thrashed, and I have no intention of making excuses. You are too generous in your victory, and I can only reply by saying that the better team won, and we know it. It was a great pleasure to hear that you enjoyed the game, for no matter what the faults in our play – and I know there were plenty – we tried our hardest to give you a good game.

I must thank you also for the way you have entertained us, providing us with a magnificient tea/dinner which we did little to deserve, but have thoroughly enjoyed.

I hear that a fixture has been arranged for a return match next month. Then we shall have the pleasure of offering you our hospitality. We hope also to avenge today's defeat. It may seem boastful to make this suggestion, after our performance today; but like most cricketers, we never know when we are beaten.

We look forward to taking the field with you again, and I share your knowledge that we are going to have another good, sporting game. On behalf of the ——— (name of club), gentlemen, I thank you.

No. 2
Toast to the Success of the Club
(SHORT TOAST)
This is generally proposed by the chairman. The speech should include tributes to the captain and other officials.

Gentlemen,

It is my duty to rise and remind you of the success the club has enjoyed during the season, and to ask you to join in drinking to continued success in the future. I am not going to spend time reviewing our achievements this season; these have been well documented, and we can feel justly proud of them. Our first eleven has won twelve matches, and lost only two.

I know you will all support me when I pay tribute to:
- Say a few words about the club secretary and officials and how they have contributed to the success of the club.
- Remind them of the excellent leadership of the captain, saying how he has been an inspiration to the team.
- Pay tribute to any individual successes, e.g. young player being chosen to play as an amateur for the County, wish him success.
- Give brief account of the club's financial position, and any changes, for example decisions to increase subscriptions.
- End on a positive note before proposing the toast.

Ours is an old club, but it is young in spirit. As I have said, we have some very promising young players; but we need more, and it is up to us older members to do our best to attract more youngsters to join us.

Now gentlemen, I ask you to join me in drinking to the future success of the club, and with this toast I couple the name of our Honorary Secretary, C ——— D ———.

REPLY

The reply to the success of the club is made by the Hon. Secretary. This speech usually ends with a toast to the captain of the club.

Mr Chairman, Gentlemen,
    Much as I appreciate the honour you have paid me of coupling my name with this toast, I feel unable to accept your compliments on my own behalf alone.

- Pay compliment to Committee teamwork.
- Add your personal support for the Captain, fine leader/ coach

    In thanking you again, therefore I ask you, gentlemen, to rise again, and drink to the health of our captain, A ———— B ————. May he have a very long innings.

NO. 3

The Gold Medallist (Golf)

This speech should be in praise of the winner of the Gold Medal (or any other award). Humour is usually appreciated on this occasion, and it is helpful to have a theme. You can then link the theme to an appropriate golf story.

Ladies and Gentlemen,
    I am very happy to propose the health of the winner of the Gold Medal.

- lead into golf story
- compliment the medallist on his outstanding performance, and propose the toast.

    He was a worthy winner, and he thoroughly deserved his success.

Gentlemen – the winner of the Gold Medal!

The following story could be used in the Gold Medallist Speech. Look out for similar stories, and adapt them to your need.

Bob Hope once told the story that his doctor told him he was overworked for a man in his eighties and needed a complete rest – and that included giving up golf. Hope decided to give up his doctor instead. He tried a second opinion and a third, and on the fourth try he found a doctor who told him he could play eighteen holes whenever he felt like it. Hope says he actually hugged the man and said 'Thanks, doc, just for that I'll remember you in my will', and the doctor said, 'In that case, play thirty-six.'

REPLY

Ladies and Gentlemen,

I feel greatly honoured by your kind reception of this toast. I do not deserve it, any more than I deserve the prize that I happen to have won. There are many golfers here who play a much better game than I do.

If possible, I am even worse at speaking than I am at golf. I have had my attack of nerves when addressing a ball, but they were nothing compared with my feelings on addressing you now. So I am going to try to hole in one, and just tell you a little story and then sit down.

– insert golf story

And with that, ladies and gentlemen, I ask you to excuse me. Again, many thanks for your kind toast.

Quotations

SPORTS

Football isn't a matter of life and death – it's much more important than that.

Bill Shankly

SPORTING TOASTS

You can't think and hit at the same time.

Yogi Berra

I hate all sports as rabidly as a person who likes sports hates common sense.

H.L. Mencken

Horses and jockeys mature earlier than people – which is why horses are admitted to race tracks at the age of two, and jockeys before they are old enough to shave.

Dick Beddoes

GOLF

Have you ever noticed what golf spells backwards?

Al Boliska

If you watch a game, it's fun. If you play it, it's recreation. If you work at it, it's golf.

Bob Hope

CRICKET

Casting a ball at three straight sticks and defending the same with a fourth.

Rudyard Kipling

If Stalin had learned to play cricket the world might now be a better place to live in.

Dr R. Downey, Archbishop of Liverpool

HORSE-RIDING

Go anywhere in England where there are natural, wholesome, contented, and really nice English people; and what do you always find? That the stables are the real centre of the household.

Lady Utterwood

SPORTING TOASTS

They say princes learn no art truly, but the art of horsemanship. The reason is, the brave beast is no flatterer. He will throw a prince as soon as his groom.

Ben Jonson

SAILING

It's like standing under a cold shower tearing up five pound notes.

Edward Heath

The Role of the Chairman

A camel looks like a horse that was planned by a committee.

Elbert Hubbard

GENERAL ADVICE

For simplicity I will use the word 'chairman' in this section. Women are just as effective in the chair as men, and today, the words 'chairperson' and 'chair' are often used at meetings.

At some time in your speaking career you may be asked to chair a meeting. This could be an important business event, or simply an informal meeting on behalf of the Parent—Teacher Association, or Board of Governors.

Whatever the purpose of the meeting, your duties as chairman are to smooth the way for both the speaker and the audience so that the meeting is an enjoyable and worthwhile occasion for all concerned. The chairman plays a vital role, and can make or break the occasion.

If you have done some public speaking before, you could well find yourself 'in the chair', and it may be useful to outline the qualities needed to do the job.

The primary quality is *Organisation*.

Before the event, the chairman should check that the speakers have received all the relevant information, particularly information relating to them. For example, how long they will speak, how questions will be handled, directions to the venue. Ask the speakers for any information which will help you prepare your introductory remarks.

He should also check that a suitable room and refreshments have been booked. (These bookings may have been made for

149

you, but it is always best to double-check!)

SEATING
For a large audience, seating will probably be theatre style, with a raised platform for the speakers. If you have more than four others on the platform with you, a simple diagram showing the seating arrangements is useful. It is customary for the speaker to be on the chairman's right. If there is more than one speaker, then they alternate, right and left.

VOTE OF THANKS (AFTER THE TALK)
Arrange to have someone give the vote of thanks after the speeches.

On the Day

- Always arrive early to check arrangements (this applies to all speaking engagements).
- Check that seating, tables, lectern, equipment are in place and in working order.

With the room set up and equipment checked out, you should then look forward to meeting the speakers. It is always a good idea to ask them to arrive half an hour or so before the event begins. You can then welcome them with coffee, and can put them at ease if they are nervous. They may also have equipment such as a projector to set up. Before you take your place in front of the audience, confirm with each speaker the length of the speech. Also check whether he wants some kind of discreet warning a few minutes before his time is up.

You may have jotted down a few introductory remarks about the speaker. Briefly talk this over with him. You may have booked him to speak some months before, and his job title/responsibilities may have altered since then, or perhaps his personal circumstances have changed, i.e. he has recently married, become a father, received an award, had a book published.

150

TIMING

Always start the meeting on time. If delay seems advisable – for example if a coach bringing a large group has broken down, but is now under way, or the first speaker has been delayed, take the audience into your confidence and suggest with their permission that you delay the start time. Your audience will appreciate being put in the picture, and will be sympathetic.

Because the duties of the chairman of a general business meeting, a public meeting or a committee have many similarities, the advice is general. Adapt it to suit your purpose. For example if your meeting involves any society business to be dealt with this should not extend into the time allotted to the speakers. If the business is short, and the information being discussed is not confidential, then you could invite the speakers to sit in.

If private, then the speaker should be made comfortable in another room. One of the group who perhaps doesn't need to be present at the meeting could entertain him. Good preparation is therefore important for successful meetings. It is the fundamental objective of successful chairmanship.

A Good Chairman will also Exercise the Following Skills:

AUTHORITY AND CONTROL

Control is important. You should keep calm and even-tempered at all times. Exercise control without appearing to dominate. Part of your job is to protect the speaker against interruption; you are the host, particularly to the speaker, generally to the audience. You are the liaison officer between them.

HUMOUR

A sense of humour is an asset. Think about the speaker in the House of Commons. By a shrewdly timed intervention he can defuse a difficult situation and regain control.

COMPETENT SPEAKING

A chairman should be a competent speaker. The tone of the meeting can be set by your opening remarks – by what you say and how you say it. It is in the opening remarks that the chairman can help a nervous speaker.

FAIRNESS
Fairness is important because people will be unhappy if they leave the meeting feeling they were denied a chance to have their say.

TACT
Tact is also a key quality. In some situations, lobbying before the meeting can be as important as what is said during the session. The chair therefore will need diplomacy when mediating between two groups.

THE SPEAKERS

Introducing the Speakers
As chairman, if you have guests to introduce, keep it brief. An introduction should last only a few minutes.

When you are ready to start, you will need to gain everyone's attention. Here are some of the methods witnessed:

- Clapping hands together.
- Banging on the table with
  - Gavel
  - Fist
  - Empty wine bottle.
- Shouting at the audience.

Remember that as chairman you should conduct yourself with decorum. Therefore, apart from the gavel, which is not always available, resist the other methods of gaining attention.

Quite simply, if you stand up and face the audience they will realise you are about to begin. Perhaps say something like 'Ladies and Gentlemen, could we now start our meeting.' Allow the audience to settle in their chairs before you start.

Introduce the speaker, but avoid clichéd phrases such as 'the speaker needs no introduction.' The obvious question is, then why are you giving one?

- Mention only those points which add gravitas to his authority to speak on his subject.
- Memorise the introduction. Be conversational, talk as you would to a friend.

Before and After the Speech

INTRODUCE THE SPEAKER
Call on the speaker by name. (Make sure you don't have to search for this). Check any unfamiliar pronunciations. Check with the speaker how he wishes to be addressed. This could be anything from just 'Jim' if he is someone already known to the group, or 'Mr James Brown', which is probably the most commonly used version, or Dr Brown if that is what the speaker prefers. With women speakers there are even more variations possible, so check their preference.

INVITE THE VOTE OF THANKS
When the speaker has sat down, the chairman should then ask the person nominated to give the vote of thanks. It should be introduced by the chairman who will 'ask Mr ——— to give the vote of thanks'.

VOTE OF THANKS BY PRE-ARRANGED PERSON
A simple vote of thanks usually makes some complimentary comments about the speaker. Start by saying that you are speaking on behalf of the audience. Even if the speech was not inspiring, try and say a few positive things about the content of the talk. Finally you propose the vote of thanks by saying something like:

Ladies and Gentlemen, on behalf of us all I would like to thank Mr ———.

You can then lead the applause and sit down.

Try to find original adjectives when giving compliments, 'an interesting talk' is sometimes taken as faint praise. If you can't think of anything, then thank the speaker for the time and effort put into the speech.

OTHER ROLES OF THE CHAIRMAN

If you are asked to chair a dinner you are, in a sense, acting as the host on behalf of the group. Your duties, as with any other chairing, are to make sure that things run smoothly and that everyone, and in particular any special guests, is kept happy. You may have to deal with any unduly rowdy behaviour or any emergency that may occur and, if you do not have a toastmaster, you will probably be expected to take on that duty as well. You must remember that your job is to be in control, but unobtrusively; you should not aim to be the star performer or outshine the guests in any way.

You will find it likely that other people will be involved in the preparatory work, such as preparing the toast list, before a dinner. However, as chairman you are normally in charge over all, so you should check that all the necessary arrangements have been made. The same level of preparation is required for this special event; leave nothing to chance. In addition to welcoming the guests and putting them at ease, you will need to liaise with the caterers. A few minutes before the meal is due to be served, you or the toastmaster should make an announcement asking everyone to move towards the tables. This is often a slow process, and you may have to make the request more than once.

Usually when the guests see the officials taking their seats they will move towards the tables. When everyone is assembled at the tables, you or the toastmaster should then knock for silence so that grace can be said. Sometimes the grace is said by a chaplain or clergyman if one is present, or by the chairman himself. If you are also acting as toastmaster, it is a good idea to ask someone else to perform this duty. If there is no grace, then the chairman should indicate the guests and officials to sit down; everyone else should follow their lead.

LINKING

Careful linking is a valuable skill for public speakers. These bridges help to ease the flow of your words and phrases. Examine the links in your final script – could your linking be improved? For example, if you are toasting guests at dinner, avoid reading out their names like a catalogue: 'We are pleased to welcome Mr Jones, Mr Smith, Mr ———.'

This is a very uninspiring welcome for guests who have perhaps travelled some distance to attend. Remember your introductions set the tone for the evening.

> We are delighted to welcome our guests this evening. Mr Jones from Surrey is with us again tonight, and from further afield, is Mr Smith from Preston.

With a bit of luck, there will be no emergencies, and you are free to relax a little during the meal, although you will probably be sitting next to the special guests and you should of course engage them in conversation.

Your official duties start again at the end of the meal with the announcement of the toasts and any after-dinner speeches. The Loyal Toast is traditionally proposed soon after the final course has been cleared away, and before the coffee. It is normally proposed by the chairman, though again if you are acting toastmaster as well you may ask someone else to propose it.

If there are other toasts to propose, there is usually a short break at this point. If you are acting as toastmaster, your duty is to knock for silence, and then introduce each toast. At the end of the dinner you will be required to round off the occasion. We said earlier that we should always try and end on a positive note. Something along the lines of:

> Well, Ladies and Gentlemen, it has been a very enjoyable/ stimulating/thought-provoking/entertaining evening and I am sure we all regret it has to come to an end so quickly.

155

THE ROLE OF THE CHAIRMAN

INTERRUPTIONS

Often, the chairman has to make announcements to the audience. If you are required to give an announcement, stand after the speaker has sat down, pause to get audience attention and make the announcement brief. Do not add to anything said by the previous speaker.

> While I am on my feet, the secretary has asked me to tell you . . .

The pause is particularly important on such occasions. By pausing and giving a few words before making the announcement, the audience will hear the message. If you simply stand up and say, 'Gentlemen, the date for the Annual Dinner/Burns Supper/ is ——', most of the audience will miss it.

The final task of the chairman is to thank the organisers. He must acknowledge them formally at the end of the event (check that you have the correct information).

CHAIRING CONFERENCES OR SIMILAR EVENTS

The chairman at a conference also needs to be well prepared. He should know all the details of arrangements and any last-minute alterations. It is particularly important that he is kept up to date with what is going on, as he will probably have delegated much of the pre-arrangements to others. In this situation, he acts as a linkman.

At a conference there are many things going on at the same time. There may be changes to timetables or syndicate rooms. The chairman is the person who normally announces these changes. He may even be asked to chair the summing-up sessions. He is on hand to offer help and support throughout the event, and may even be on duty in the evenings when delegates are relaxing over drinks. A distinct advantage for this type of chairman would be the ability to speak off the cuff and make quick decisions, as he will not know beforehand how events may turn out.

156

COMPÈRING

A slightly different kind of linkman is the compère. More and more companies are using the 'master of ceremonies' technique in both business and social activities. Increasing numbers of organisations engage a Public Relations company to organise this, particularly for large events.

Most entertainment events need someone to be in control. If you are asked to undertake such a role, your function is to introduce the acts, and to try to keep the audience happy if there are any snags. The number one rule here is to remember that the audience are there for the entertainment and not to listen to you. By now you will be familiar with the expression 'keep it brief'.

Don't try to be funny, particularly if you are introducing professional comedians. A humorous anecdote, however, may go down well if you need to keep the audience amused while backstage problems are being dealt with. If there is a major delay, then it is best to go on stage and explain the problem. You could add an assurance that the act will be well worth waiting for. If necessary you may need to appear again to give a progress report. If there is a major problem, then the audience will appreciate being told.

Some years ago, I was sitting in a packed London theatre when the action on the stage came to an abrupt halt. The actors, swords drawn, froze where they stood. The theatre manager leapt onto the stage and shouted out that well-worn cliché, 'Is there a doctor in the house?'

Someone rushed forward from the back of the theatre to attend the member of the audience who had been taken ill. After what seemed like an eternity, but which was probably less than five minutes, the unfortunate man was carried out of the theatre, apparently none the worse for his dilemma. His friend called out as they left, 'Please continue.'

During this action, the packed theatre was stunned into silence; you could have heard a pin drop. The manager again took the stage, and said, 'Ladies and Gentlemen, with your permission we would like to continue where we left off'. To a tumultuous applause, the cast carried out the finale as if nothing had happened.

Although serious at the time, I look back on this incident with amusement. The lesson is that in an emergency, the audience will not riot if there is a change of plan.

Chairman's Checklist

- Be well prepared before the event.
- Be punctual. Start meetings on time.
- Be fair and tactful.
- Be firm. Keep control of the occasion.
- Know the formal (also unwritten) rules of your organisation.
- Check all your facts before introducing speakers. Keep the introduction brief.
- Gain audience attention before you introduce the speakers.
- 'Protect' speakers if the meeting gets out of hand.
- Ensure the audience can hear questions being answered. Repeat or clarify these if required.
- Develop a system of cues for your support staff. For example, turning out lights for slide presentation, handing out support materials.
- Keep to the agreed agenda, and don't allow speakers to go over time.
- Thank the organisers.

Tips

- Be aware of your body language – give the speaker eye contact now and again, also glance at the audience and look interested. The audience will often take their cue from the chairman. The speaker will also be aware of your reactions so aim for active listening, this will help support him if he's feeling nervous.
- As part of your preparation make a 'what if' list. This is a useful device for all speaking occasions. It is a common fear amongst speakers that something may go wrong. For example, what if . . . I dry up, lose the place, drop my notes, miss a slide? This is unlikely, but it has been known to happen.

A 'what if' list is simply a contingency plan should things go wrong. On more than one occasion I have arrived at a venue to speak, where the equipment asked for, an overhead projector or flipchart, is not available. A contingency plan might be to prepare your overhead slides, but also to be able to give the talk without them. I have also experienced broken and incomplete equipment, such as a broken projector lamp, or a flipchart without marker pens (or dry pens). A contingency here might be to carry a set of pens with you if you intend using a flipchart. Keep your list simple and vary it for each occasion. Here are a few broad headings; add your own.

What if?	Contingency
Personal	
Material	
Venue/Equipment	
Late Speaker	
Speaker called off	
Catering arrangements	
Excessive heckling from audience*	
Small audience turnout (see below)	

*See chapter on Any Questions. (page 164)

APOLOGIES FOR A SMALL AUDIENCE
There is nothing more embarrassing than inviting a guest speaker along to speak to your organisation, membership or club and then finding that, for whatever reason, the audience is pathetically small.

- Make your apologies as best you can, relying on the atrocious weather conditions, tube strike, bomb scare, or any other excuse that seems reasonable.
- If possible transfer to a smaller room. A small audience is lost in a large room. If this is not possible, ask your audience to move down to the front rows.
- Adapt your introduction to the occasion. (If you have been super efficient in your preparation you will have anticipated

a low turnout, and added it to your 'what if' list.)

You may say something along these lines:

Distinguished Guests, Ladies and Gentlemen,
    I know that we will all be sorry that this atrocious snow storm has kept so many people away. But all is not lost, we are to have a treat this evening, for we have among us one of the most distinguished politicians/one of the most eminent scientists/one of the top industrialists.
    We have gathered here because we know of the work of our guest speaker, and on behalf of us all, I welcome him to ———.

Then give details about the guest, and round off your introduction:

Ladies and Gentlemen, I present Mr ———.

Booking and Briefing Speakers

Some people think that speaking, like sex, ought to come to us all naturally. Maybe it should; but in both cases it's just as well to learn a few tricks.

Lord Mancroft

Booking

The eternal problem of function organisers is finding speakers.

Successful speakers are always in demand, and after-dinner speakers are usually engaged by reputation being passed on. A guest hears a speaker in Birmingham and buttonholes him to see if he can travel to London for another society. That is usually the way it happens. Your committee or selection board should be composed of men and women who move around the social, political and business fields, and know a good speaker when they hear one. The speaker should be selected with care, matching the speaker with the audience.

If you need three speakers for an event, if possible get three members of your committee to choose one each. If one member is left to make the decisions, you may get speakers cast in the same mould, simply because the member has a personal preference for such speakers. The evening will then lack variety and be as dull as taking eight national anthems for your Desert Island Discs.

So, if you need three speakers to follow your chairman, choose a strong one to follow your chairman's opening speech. Put the less experienced (or most nervous) in the middle, and leave the most humorous to last. If you can avoid it don't put outstanding or very funny speakers on early, they may be hard acts to follow.

161

BOOKING AND BRIEFING SPEAKERS

What if the speaker has to cancel the speaking engagement? Committees engaging amateur speakers should always lay on a standby, perhaps someone from their own ranks. Inviting amateur speakers involves no contracts, just goodwill, so the possibility of last minute cry-offs must be covered.

If, in booking speakers, organisers used a professional agent, then he would find substitute speakers as part of the contract.

Briefing

Organisers of functions should *always* brief speakers by letter. Initial contact is often made by phone, but always follow this up with something in writing. Many functions have been ruined by the guest speaker turning up on the wrong date, or at the wrong venue. Which recalls the famous telegram G.K. Chesterton sent to his wife after setting out on a speaking date . . . 'Am at Aylesbury – where should I be?' Write personally to speakers and make sure you include the following information:

- Venue, time of reception, informal or black tie.
- Printed invitation/ticket (this usually has more information).
- Include any information to help prepare speech: his objectives for the evening – the toast he is to propose.
- Information about your society/organisation/company.
- Ask for speaker details; for example, how he would like to be billed, and how he would like to be announced.
- If staying overnight, details of hotel.
- Include all telephone numbers.
- Give the speaker a deadline to accept your invitation to speak, and ask for his acceptance in writing.

The professional speaker, VIP or star may have been booked to speak for half an hour or more, but most amateurs will be on their feet for less than ten minutes. If you can avoid it, don't ask speakers to travel long distances to speak for five or ten minutes. Local speakers are best used here.

I remember one extremely entertaining actress being left with a mere six minutes before an audience had to rush off for the last train. She had travelled some distance, was giving her services and yet the previous local monopolists ate into her time. The audience were furious with the weak chairman who allowed this to happen.

In these circumstances, if you feel that local speakers may go over their time, then perhaps a better plan would be to confine the evening entirely to the chairman's opening address followed by the main speaker, and close with a vote of thanks from the chair. If you are fortunate to have a very good speaker then there is no need to overload with others.

Any Questions?

GENERAL ADVICE

Many types of speeches involve taking questions from the audience. You may have decided to ask for questions during the talk or afterwards. If you have a chairman, and there is more than one speaker, the format will be decided for you. In this case you will probably be asked to take part in a panel session after the speeches are over. This simply means that all the speakers sit facing the audience, and questions to individual speakers are directed through the chair.

Many novice speakers dread this part of the proceedings almost as much as giving the speech itself. The main fears centre around the feeling of being out of control, and a feeling of vulnerability (you can be asked anything, and even worse – you may not know the answer). Fortunately, these fears vanish if you think of the question-and-answer session as something you can control.

To Keep Control

- Set the ground rules for questions.
- Limit the kind of questions: 'I will be dealing with questions relating to the subject I have covered.'
- Keep control by moving closer into the audience.
- Remain standing and give good eye contact.
- Show confidence by laying down your notes and giving the audience your full attention.
- If you are taking questions at the end, reserve the last few moments for yourself: 'I'd be happy to answer any questions, but I would like to hold the last few minutes for a summary.'

  If you do this you can recover from a particularly awkward last question by leaving the audience with your positive note.

164

ANY QUESTIONS?

It may surprise you to know that speakers look and often feel more at ease when answering questions, mainly because their defences are down. The spotlight is off them to perform, and they can concentrate on the needs of the audience.

Question time should be of mutual benefit to both speaker and audience. A common fear is that they won't be asked any questions.

> Edinburgh is a very flourishing city
>
> Margaret Thatcher
> (on a visit to Scotland, and being asked a
> question about the economy.)

There are a number of alternatives to 'answering questions'. While some of the following may be too extreme for normal use, and all are only appropriate for specific circumstances, we should never forget their existence. Many politicians have survived on them for years.

- Throw the question to the audience.
- Throw the question back to the questioner.
- Throw the question to a colleague.
- Admit you don't know (but say you will find out).
- Postpone an answer until later in the talk.
- Give clues that will help the questioner to develop his own answer.
- Answer a different question.
- Waffle meaninglessly.
- Refuse to answer (with or without an excuse).
- Feign illness or death.

Anticipate Questions

When analysing your expected audience, try to anticipate the kind of questions you will be asked, and also possible objections. Knowing a little about your audience (audience profile), means that you can examine your speech to see if what you have

165

to say could cause doubt, disbelief or controversy.

When Questions Come – Listen to Your Audience

$X + Y + Z = SUCCESS$. This is the formula Dr Albert Einstein recommends for success. When X represents hard work, Y represents play, and Z represents 'the ability to keep your mouth shut and listen'.

Listen in this case to the questions and comments from your audience. This means more than hearing or appearing attentive. It means being actively absorbed in what is being said, gaining clear insight into what is meant and what is implied and into why it was expressed in one way rather than another. Skilled listening on your part will help others to be objective and keep the discussion on target. It is also essential in encouraging participation.

As well as being the speaker, there are times in the presentation where you will take on the role of listener. Listening skills can be divided into two categories: passive and active.

Often we fail to pick up the messages on the emotional line, or we may pick them up, but pretend not to and ignore them. We may be so emotionally involved that we fail to hear what is said. If the gap between words and emotions (head and heart) is small, the message will be received. If, however, the gap is large, the listener will be confused.

The major processes of active listening fall into four areas: interpreting, observing, reflecting data and reflecting feeling.

INTERPRETING

Sometimes it is appropriate to interpret what the speaker is saying. However, be careful of negative reaction from the person who has asked the question. He may feel that you are deliberately distorting the intended message for undeclared reasons of your own. Giving attention to your questioners helps them off-load negative feelings and experiences which get in the way of clear thinking and effective action. Active listening should not be seen as a mere technique for influence. It is only useful in influencing if the listener is generally attentive and

166

values the other individual's point of view.

OBSERVING

Careful, non-evaluative attention and eye contact while listening automatically aids the speaker to express what he wishes to say. This provides a warm, accepting atmosphere for the speaker's thoughts, ideas, attitudes and values. Observation tunes the listener in to the speaker's words and the emotional 'music' which accompanies them, often revealed by facial expressions and body language.

REFLECTING DATA

This process, often referred to as 'paraphrasing' is akin to holding a mirror in front of the speaker, reflecting back phrases as you hear them. This increases clarity and lets the speaker know that you are hearing accurately.

REFLECTING FEELING

As you become familiar with the questioner's emotions and the 'music' behind the words, reflecting them back will test your perceptions, as well as giving information and feedback to the questioner about his feelings. This is particularly useful if words and emotions seem incongruous. Reflecting feelings provides continual testing and expressing of understanding.

Listen carefully to what is actually said, right to the end. There is always the danger of listening only at the start, and thus failing to grasp what is really being asked. This applies particularly if we are anxious about possible hostile questions: it is easy to assume a questioner is being critical when he is actually being supportive.

Key Points to Answering Questions

REPEAT

Repetition is legitimate if everyone did not hear the original question (e.g. if it was asked from the front row), to eliminate misunderstanding, or, provided it is not too obvious, to play for time. We can repeat the exact words, to check we have heard, or paraphrase, to check we have understood.

BE COURTEOUS
However we feel inside, we should indicate our appreciation that the questioner has taken the trouble to explore our thinking. We should thank the questioner explicitly for his question, say that he has raised an interesting point, or simply smile and use some turn of phrase to convey appreciation.

We should always adopt this approach even if we believe the question is particularly stupid, or has been fully covered in what we have just said. If this situation is not handled correctly, the audience will likely take the side of the questioner and will dismiss the speaker as being rude or egotistical. It is amazing what interest and hidden significance can be found behind a silly question if we really try. Particularly if the question comes from an influential member of the audience.

SEPARATE
Multi-part questions are often asked, and it is always best to disentangle them and answer each part separately, answering the easiest first.

ASSUMPTIONS
Beware of assumptions. It is possible, particularly when involved in controversy, to be drawn into accepting an assumption without realising it. Always review the assumption behind a question before attempting an answer, and if necessary challenge it politely but firmly.

EXERCISE CONTROL
If aggressive or personal questions are asked (and this will be much rarer than we fear), then coolness under fire is essential. It is often possible to ignore unpleasant innuendos, while still answering the main question. A touch of humour can defuse many situations, if we have the gift for it. Sarcasm, however, must never be used.

Heckling is rarely experienced outside political meetings. If you find yourself in this situation, keep cool and don't lose your temper, or the hecklers will have won.

The best weapon against heckling is quick wit. Without being spiteful or malicious, try to get the audience to laugh with you at the expense of the heckler. (They are usually only a small minority in the audience.)

An example of brilliant repartee was given by George Bernard Shaw when he made the 'curtain' speech on the first night of one of his plays. The final curtain was the signal for great applause and the usual cries of 'Author!' When Shaw appeared, the audience further showed its approval of the play by applauding still more loudly. Then, as the clapping and cheering died down, a single but very loud boo came down from the gallery. Shaw looked up and said: 'I quite agree with you, sir – but what are we two against so many who hold a different opinion?'

BE TRUTHFUL

You have been asked to speak because you know a lot about your subject. But there may be a few occasions when you will not be able to give a factual answer. If caught out, the only sensible strategy is to own up immediately and with as little embarrassment as possible. (Say you will find out for them, and do so. Also anticipate this question when next you give the same talk.)

There is also an alternative strategy if you don't know an answer. This will depend on many things, but would be suitable at a fairly informal occasion, such as a presentation to professionals who are experts in their own field, e.g. medical/law/finance/computer technology. You may be asked a question you can't answer, but perhaps someone in the audience would know. (Your audience won't expect you to know everything.) In this case, say something like: 'I'm sorry I don't have that information to hand, but perhaps someone else here might know?' Pose the question to the audience and pause for reaction. Chances are that someone will come up with that date/statistics/product name/number. Members of an audience, particularly of specialists, are always willing to share their knowledge with others.

169

ANY QUESTIONS?

TIMING

Good answers are usually neither too long nor too short. If an answer appears simple and short, it may be courteous and helpful to expand it, with appropriate backgound.

On the other hand, the speaker should not go on too long, or use the question time as an opportunity to throw in irrelevant material he forgot to use in his speech.

It is unusual for the request, 'Are there any questions?' to be met with silence. If it should happen, there are usually two simple reasons:

- You have covered all the potential questions during your talk, or
- Your audience feel uncomfortable, or don't feel emotionally involved.

Some Hints

Hand out question cards at the beginning of the presentation. This gives people a chance to jot down thoughts as they occur. If you ask them to do this, remind them to keep the questions short and to write clearly. This method is particularly useful for large and formal presentations.

This method also works successfully with small groups. The questions could be taken from the audience and written on the flipchart, to be answered at the end of the session.

METHOD

- Before beginning the presentation, ask if there are any specific questions the audience would like answered before they leave that day. (Often people attend these occasions in order to get answers to specific questions.)
- Keep requests short – write on the flipchart using key words.
- Eliminate any questions which you know are covered in your talk. (Only use this method if it is a small group, i.e. under ten people.) You should spend only a few minutes writing up, otherwise it's too time-consuming. Many presenters use this method as it breaks the ice with the audience before they

begin their presentation, and also it is a motivating force for the audience to know that they will leave having had their important questions answered.

- Often at large gatherings people are invited for coffee before the event. This is also a good time to do the list, or get them to do it. If you decide not to use the list, then at least circulate and chat with the members of your audience. By doing this you will be able to gauge the content of questions likely to be asked.
- Mention the list as part of your introduction when you would normally mention questions. For example INTRO: your name, background, structure etc . . . then . . . motion to flipchart.

Thank you, ladies and gentlemen for these questions. I have allocated about thirty minutes for questions at the end of the presentation, by which time, I'm sure you'll have many more.

OTHER METHODS

- Arrange with the programme chairman to select a member of the audience ahead of time to ask the first question; or ask a colleague sitting in the audience to ask a pre-arranged one, one which will elicit a response from the rest of the group. Be aware that if using this method, an obviously 'rehearsed' question could lose you credibility. (This is a favoured method at large meetings.)
- Take an information survey (which you have worked out in advance) and ask for a show of hands. The results of a simple question such as 'How many of you feel we need to improve our corporate video?' can give you new information to discuss and also gets the audience involved. This type of question can also act as an ice-breaker.
- In a large group, few people want to ask the first question. To get over this you could pose a rhetorical question, and if you also make it provocative, you are likely to get a response.

171

DEFENSIVENESS

Never be defensive, and never retaliate. No matter how rude and offensive the questioner, stay calm. If you have built up a good relationship with your audience, they will support you. I have seen a supportive audience use peer pressure to silence a hostile questioner who was intent on being heard.

TAKE RESPONSIBILITY

Don't embarrass a questioner, even if it is clear that he hasn't been listening. Avoid saying things like, 'I've covered that already, weren't you listening?' Rather, take the responsibility yourself:

'I'm sorry, perhaps I didn't explain that clearly.'

PUBLIC EXECUTION

Never take a person on in public. This is embarrassing for everyone. Keep calm, and suggest you speak in private later. I recall an occasion where a sales manager was belittled in front of his colleagues by an officious and arrogant speaker. The speaker believed in the old adage, 'attack is the best form of defence'. He let rip on the manager, made a few irrelevant comments and carried on with his talk.

This speaker had spent no time beforehand speaking with the group or establishing any warmth. This was evident at lunch, which followed on from this incident. The chastened manager was joined by his peers, and the speaker dined alone.

If you are asked a question which is clearly argumentative ask the individual to expand on his concern. You might say, 'Can you tell me a little more about why you feel that way about . . .?' By keeping the would-be arguer talking, you frequently unearth hidden attitudes or agenda not evident in the questions as posed.

OBJECTIONS

These can arise in any speaking situation where the audience is participative, i.e. able to ask questions, give opinions etc. In these circumstances, whatever the merits of your idea, you can probably expect someone to present arguments as to why it should not be adopted. You should be prepared to answer these questions. The rules that apply to questions also apply to objections. Play the devil's advocate with yourself: think of the strongest possible argument against your point of view and cover it in your presentation. If you are challenged, introduce a telling argument in the idea's favour. Later, when a more positive tone has been built up again, you can refer back to the argument and neutralise it further with a few positive statements. Avoid a controversial attitude at all costs. An argumentative or defensive approach creates the impression that you are not quite sold on your own ideas.

In general you should listen, not be defensive, and acknowledge the objector's point of view: 'I never thought of it like that; thank you for your thought.'

When objections to your ideas are raised, you can turn them to your own advantage if you encourage the person who raised the objection to expand or elaborate. Frequently, the more one talks, the weaker the objection becomes. Even when the objection is irrelevant, you should stay calm. Careful listening enables you to determine whether the objection has any relevant bearing on your idea, or whether the intention is simply to reduce your stature.

Another ploy is to ask questions with which the person who raised the objection has to agree. Where applicable, a series of such questions invariably shrivels the objection and terminates in a sound conclusion with which the objector is forced to agree. This technique needs much thought and skill beforehand. A well-tried method, particularly with sales people is the 'three Fs' technique – Feel, Felt and Found.

For example, answering an objection to cost:

I understand why you may feel that way (empathy). Many of our customers felt that way in the beginning . . . but they found that . . . (benefits gained) . . . This computer software package actually saved them money in the long run (testimonial).

This method is particularly potent if you can name a satisfied client and cite actual benefits gained as examples.

Try not to reject objections or suggestions that would improve your idea. Even if somebody suggests something that, in your mind, would add nothing significant to your ideas, do not reject them out of hand. After you have presented your ideas, arrange for a break, followed if possible by a discussion period.

The break will enable listeners to sort through various impressions and questions that occurred to them. During the final discussion period you should sum up the salient points of your ideas, i.e. the anticipated benefits and advantages, the need that exists or can be created for the idea, the reasons for immediate implementation of the idea.

It is most important to gain the enthusiasm of those who will develop and execute your idea. If your associates and staff, as well as your superiors, are not convinced of its value, it may fail.

Problem Behaviour

Every speaking situation, whether it is a committee meeting, business or after-dinner, provides opportunity for non-productive behaviour.

DOMINATING

This type of behaviour can often happen when the chairman 'pulls rank'. Seniority often predominates.

BLOCKING

Any action which interferes with the progress of the group. Examples of this would be a speaker deliberately getting off the subject; recounting personal experiences which are irrelevant to the subject; the after-dinner speaker deliberately taking up more than his alloted time or the committee member who always takes a negative approach, i.e. 'We tried that before and it didn't work.'

AGGRESSION

Occurs when a member blames others for his own mistakes, showing hostility to individuals or groups, attaching motives to

174

others. Deflating the self-image of others: 'If you had completed the report on schedule we would have won the order.'

SEEKING STATUS

Drawing attention by boasting, talking in an aggressive manner, using distracting dress or mannerisms. 'At ———, we always do it this way.'

SPECIAL PLEADING

Going 'all out' to get a point across. Often this person will have hidden motives or a hobby-horse. These may be used to cloud the issue and to support their point of view: 'All my divisional directors'/'The average public speaker'/'Most experienced chairmen'.

MANIPULATING

Attempting to control the group by pulling strings or rank. Frequent resort to name-dropping. Tends to divide the group into cliques.

Remember, if you are in the chair it is down to you to protect your guests from any problem behaviour from the audience. This is where the chairman may 'dominate' the culprit and pull him into line, provided it is done with courtesy.

If there is no chairman, then the speaker is in control. He must firmly assume responsibility for the situation.

Use Your Audience

Many problem situations can be handled by involving your audience. Get them on your side. They are all too well aware of the person who gets on his hobby-horse and monopolises question time. Use your body to block them off.

This is one occasion when you should forget 'full frontals', and stand 'side on' to the questioner. Don't give them eye contact, and ask a question of someone else: 'Let's hear someone else's opinion.'

The chairman is there to help you, but really shouldn't have to step in. If you are given the privilege of standing up and speaking to an audience, then you are in charge.

ANY QUESTIONS?

Assert confidence from the minute you open your mouth to speak.

Questions and Answer Checklist

- Anticipate and prepare possible questions and objections. (Check your audience profile.)
- Truly listen. This is an essential skill for a successful presenter.
- Maintain your credibility and control.
- Stay calm at all times – don't be defensive.
- Treat your audience as individuals.
- Welcome questions – be warm and friendly.
- Give the audience full attention – display positive body language.
- Answer the questions briefly and stop.
- Give good eye contact: 80% to the questioner and 20% to the rest of the audience.
- Recognise questions in order. When more than one questioner has his hand up, mentally note the first, and deal with the others in order.
- If asking questions of the audience, initially direct questions to the whole group (shotgun approach). Follow with questions to individuals (rifle approach). This avoids putting members of the audience 'on the spot'.

Other Types of
Speaking Situations

IMPROMPTU SPEAKING

It takes more than three weeks to prepare a good impromptu
speech.

Mark Twain

Have you ever been in a business or social meeting when
someone has surprised you with the words, 'And now . . . will
stand up and speak to us for a few minutes about . . .?' Or
'. . . , you attended the AGM/Conference/Seminar, would you
like to say a few words about it?'

This is referred to as an impromptu speech, one in which you
must talk without preparation time, without notes, and entirely
from recall. A terrifying situation; as you hear your name, your
heart beats faster, your mind goes blank!

Thinking 'on your feet' is not as difficult as it may seem if you
can master a few guidelines that can also apply to a prepared
speech.

Five-point Plan for Impromptu Speaking

- Quickly formulate the general purpose of your talk. Are you
  going to ask for action, inform, persuade?
- Next, consider your listeners' objectives.
- Use the simple prompts, who, why, where, when, how, to
  build up your talk.
- Do they need more data – if so, what? Should they feel
  differently – how? Should they take action – when?

- Choose some mental prompts which will serve as key words.

Another useful device is to build on the previous speaker's comments or briefly summarise what has been said and add your own views.

EXTEMPORANEOUS SPEAKING

This differs from the above, in that this speech appears to be made spontaneously, but is, in fact, carefully prepared. It sounds as if it has been made 'off the cuff'. Winston Churchill brought this technique to a fine art.

For most people, it is extremely difficult to memorise a speech and then to present it, word for word extemporaneously. There is the constant danger that if you forget one key word, you will lose your ideas, continuity and spontaneity. One way of overcoming this is to learn to speak from ideas alone – from personal experience and knowledge; then the words will come. If you have a good memory, you can memorise the general outline of the speech, and a few key words on cards should suffice.

Both the impromptu and extemporaneous speech should include the other vital ingredients to make them a success: enthusiasm and vitality!

THE LECTURE

The lecture is a popular method of putting across information when large groups of people are involved. There are certain *advantages* to this method:

- It is an effective way to present material to large groups.
- It can be used to give the outline or background to a very broad subject, of which the details can be given later by other speaking techniques; for example in small group

talks, discussion groups, using supporting material such as reports and papers.

- It can allow large quantities of material to be presented very quickly.

The *disadvantages* are:

- The audience is not involved. If the presenter does not actively attempt to keep the attention level high, then the audience will lose interest. This is made more difficult because of the volume of information which is being presented.
- There is no feedback. The presenter does not know if she is on the right track, or if the audience is taking in the information being put across.

Hints on Preparing a Lecture

- Know your objectives and those of your audience.
- Research your audience and your material.
- Have a clear structure to your lecture.
- Hook the audience attention in the opening and emphasise the key points. Tell them what's in it for them.
- Check that your verbals and non-verbals match up. Be enthusiastic about your topic.
- Be aware of the non-verbal communication of your audience. Be prepared to change the pace if, for example, the audience is getting restless or looks bored.
- Maintain interest by including humour, anecdotes, examples, visuals, as appropriate.
- Summarise frequently.
- End on a high – a 'positive' note.

The lecture provides an excellent opportunity to use visual aids. For example, you may be delivering a travel lecture to a social group, or a lecture on art to the local art club. In this case the use of 35mm slides or video is ideal. If you intend using visuals, then see the section on Visual Aids (page 32). When using 35mm slides, it is customary to use them in a darkened or semi-darkened room.

OTHER TYPES OF SPEAKING SITUATIONS

This has the disadvantage of the speaker not being able to see the audience.

Here are some additional hints on planning this type of talk.

TO AVOID CONDUCTING THE WHOLE LECTURE IN A DARKENED ROOM

- Prepare to deliver the introduction to your talk with all the lights on. Come out front into the audience, and introduce yourself and your subject. Give them some background information about what they are about to see.
- Having made contact with your audience in this way, you could then switch off some of the lights and go through your slide show, explaining as necessary. If someone is working your audio visuals, check cues with them.
- When using visuals, always rehearse before the event.
- Switch on the lights again for your summing up. You may want also to take questions at this point.

I have attended this type of talk where the speaker has started and ended his talk in almost total darkness. The audience likes to see the speaker, and a nice friendly introduction will make the lecture more enjoyable for all concerned.

Summary of the Lecture/Talk

- Never start your speaking career in this field. Gain experience with other 'speech' audiences first.
- You must be an expert in your subject.
- Adjust your material to match your audience.
- Make any notes of questions posed to you after your talk so that you can add these to future talks.
- Give your talks self-explanatory titles, clear and bold.
- Avoid blinding with science.
- Use discretion when using visual aids.
- Arrive in time to check equipment.
- Play down your qualifications and experience. Rely on your performance to establish your expertise.

OTHER TYPES OF SPEAKING SITUATIONS

THE TECHNICAL PRESENTATION

Technical professionals are often let down by poor speaking skills. They may be talented and knowledgeable in technical areas, but are often bypassed for promotion by less efficient colleagues who speak well in public.

As well as adhering to the general rules for preparation, the technical specialist needs to take particular care when deciding what level of detail is required by the audience. All too often the technical presentation can sink in a morass of technical detail and jargon. Examine your audience carefully. For example, you may be asked to give an informative talk to the local Rotary Club on the latest information technology. Although your audience will consist of intelligent business people, don't assume that they know even the basics about the subject.

Simple words that are common in the world of computing and communications are not always understood by the general public. Another audience may be a gathering of technical staff. You may be part of a group presentation, where you provide the technical expertise.

Six-point Plan for the Technical Talk

- Often this type of talk includes a product presentation. Take extra care in rehearsals. Practise with all equipment in situ, and work out a contingency plan in the event of equipment breakdown.
- Briefly explain any technical jargon which you will use.
- Encourage questions throughout the talk. This will enable the audience to clarify any points that are unclear.
- Keep the information short and punchy. Give the minimum detail to meet your objectives.
- Allow a reasonable time for questions at the end.
- Support your talk by giving out leaflets, brochures, information about the subject. Give these out at the end of the speech.

181

OTHER TYPES OF SPEAKING SITUATIONS

TALKS TO FOREIGN GROUPS

When giving talks to foreign groups, where English is not the first language:

- If possible, allow for some tuning-in time where the listeners can tune in to your voice, your intonation and your accent.
- Use short words and sentences. Many foreigners have a higher level of proficiency in the reading of English than they have in the spoken language.
- To maximise understanding, put only one idea into each sentence. Speak clearly, and give the audience time to digest the information.
- Break up the information. Remember that information
  - introduced on a 'quick fix' basis = confusion
  - poorly paced = uninteresting
  - too much, too soon = information overload.
- Pace yourself carefully. Pause at the end of each sentence or phrase. Your audience then has time to catch up and digest the information.
- Avoid technical terms, jargon, slang and clichés.
- Use active sentence structures.
- Research shows that approximately 78% of the English language, as it is used in daily life, is composed of active sentence structures. For example: 'We evaluated (active verb) the reaction of the audience' instead of: 'Audience reactions were evaluated' (passive verb).
- Put important information at the end of a sentence and never at the beginning.

Different Cultures

You may be asked to speak abroad, or have the pleasure of addressing an audience of guests from all over the world. The language you use is important, take care not to offend. Often a similar word has a different meaning in another country. For example, if speaking to an audience from the USA, asking for a rubber would certainly raise an eyebrow; 'He was my fag at Eton' would raise two!

182

OTHER TYPES OF SPEAKING SITUATIONS

BAR MITZVAH

Speech-making at a bar mitzvah is very ritualised and formula speeches are the appropriate address at the synagogue. Speeches at the party afterwards are a matter of choice and are more open to personal interpretation.

A SIMPLE FORMAT

- A short speech of thanks – thanking guests for attending.
- Congratulations to the child on coming of age, wishing them well in their adult life and in the continuation of their Jewish studies (made by the child's father).

REPLY TO ABOVE
The bar mitzvah should respond briefly by acknowledging the first speech and thanking his family as well as those responsible for his religious education.

UNIVERSITY GRADUATION PARTY

This is becoming a popular family celebration. The main theme is to applaud the graduate's achievements, and acknowledge the supportive parents.

- It is customary for the father to give brief congratulations to the graduate. He should acknowledge any past teachers or lecturers who are present and any relatives or friends who have had a special influence.
- The graduate should then respond by thanking the parents for their material and emotional support (also mentioning any other siblings).
- The closing speech should be made by a close friend of the graduate. This can be a very light-hearted, humorous speech, and should conclude by reinforcing the message of gratitude to the parents.

183

OTHER TYPES OF SPEAKING SITUATIONS

VISITING DELEGATIONS

This group may come from another town or from overseas. Speakers may be asked to make a speech at a reception for the visitors.

The speakers should plan this speech with a view to:

- Paying tribute to the country or town.
- Mentioning the sport, team, activity, e.g. history of art in Italy, football in Brazil, golf in Scotland.

The aim in this type of speech is to welcome the visitors and pay them the compliment of having taken the trouble to find out something about their country and customs.

Encyclopaedias are useful resources to find information on countries, but they are often a year or so out of date. The appropriate embassy or consulate will yield more up-to-date information.

FUNERALS

Funerals and burials have always been important ceremonial rituals, no matter what culture or religion. On this occasion, simplicity is the key. To be asked to perform this task is a great act of trust from the bereaved family, either to one of its own members or a friend. It may be delivered at the graveside, in a church, a crematorium chapel, or sometimes at home.

The clergyman will most likely have given an address at one of those places, and if he knew the deceased may well have spoken personally about him. If this is the case, then check with the clergyman beforehand that your eulogy does not overlap. Conversational tone is recommended, and if you are speaking outside, be prepared to speak slightly louder than you might do indoors. Some hints:

184

- Speak from a prepared text:
  Format
  - Opening (perhaps open with a quotation or part of a psalm which was a favourite of the deceased).
  - Follow this with a short chronological account of the deceased's life. Mention their birth, education, marriage, family, war service, work, recreational activities, clubs they belonged to etc.
  - A telling anecdote is appropriate; choose one which is flattering. Also include something of their values, such as '——— was a wonderful father/loving grandfather.'
- If the death was the result of a protracted illness, you could acknowledge this by saying something like '———'s health had declined over the last few years.' You could then make some comment about how they coped bravely. Check this statement out with members of the family who sometimes cannot bear any reference to illness.
- The conclusion should be a tribute to the surviving partner and/or members of the family in their time of sorrow.

COMPETITIVE PRESENTATIONS

Professional services are offered by a growing number of consultants. We live in competitive times and the nature of the consultancy business means that time is money. To help you formulate your approach for this type of presentation use the 3 P's: Preparation, Professionalism and Persistency.

PREPARATION

This stage should come automatically now. Time and effort spent beforehand is the rule. Growing numbers of competitors in all market sectors are competing for business.

To win this, you have to be better than your competition. Companies expect consultants to understand their market, their business and their problems. The following checklist will help you through your planning.

OTHER TYPES OF SPEAKING SITUATIONS

Imagine that you have managed to obtain a meeting with —————— company. They have asked you along to see what you have to offer in the way of services/products etc.

- Before the meeting, request information about the company: annual report, brochures, newsletters, sales literature.
- Know who you will be talking with at the meeting, their position in the company, and if possible their role in the decision-making process. Ask if they are speaking with other consultants. Potential clients are often willing to divulge this information. However, don't be surprised if they are coy about telling you who else is in the frame. Clients often don't like divulging this information until ready to make a choice.
- Try and define the objectives, i.e. what is the client looking for. Initially this can be difficult – the client often prefers to let the consultant 'do the talking' with the minimum of input from them. At this stage the client is sounding the consultant out, and gauging if the chemistry is right between them. Listen carefully to what is being said. Look for connections. How might you be able to help?

  If you have any recommendations at this stage you may want to suggest them. It may still not be clear what the client is looking for, so when making recommendations keep them flexible; if possible offer alternatives.
- Take along some of your own work; literature, references, case histories which show your professionalism.
- Personal presentation (see section on Dress, page 48). Remember you represent your company, so be smart and business-like.

PROFESSIONALISM
This must be apparent to the client from the beginning or they will not take the matter further.

- Show an interest in the company. Ask questions and make it clear that you have done your homework. Use questioning techniques to elicit information, which will help you identify the root problem as quickly as possible.

- Show a grasp and understanding of the client's actual situation and in the early stages make a 'pass' at a solution to demonstrate competence. Agree on the next stage, which is likely to be a written proposal from you.
- Use a systematic approach. Put as much effort into this stage as you would into a formal presentation. Research and prepare thoroughly. The written proposal should look good and read well: use clear language and focus on the client, identifying the present situation, making the proposal and outlining the benefits to the client.
- If it has gone well up to this stage you may be invited back either to sign a contract, or to make a formal presentation of your proposal. At the end of the day the client may change the brief, or say, 'I'll think about it.'
- If you have made a good presentation, then you have a better chance of winning the business.

PERSISTENCY

Success in part goes to those who are persistent, who follow up confidently and who, when successful, maintain a good client relationship.

NOTE

If you are asked to do a client presentation then the use of overhead slides is advisable. The slides should be personalised for the client company.

Correct Form

This is a very complicated area, which could take a whole book dedicated to the subject. Never guess the correct form of address. If you are in any doubt always check. Your local library will have information, or ask advice of someone who has delivered the speech before. The following are some forms of address which are most commonly encountered.

Royalty

Her Majesty the Queen

When the Sovereign is present a speech should start: 'May it please Your Majesty, Mr Chairman . . .' etc.

If during the speech you address the Queen directly, on the first occasion, one says 'Your Majesty'. Further direct address is 'Ma'am'. (The same address applies to Queen Elizabeth, The Queen Mother.)

The title of 'Majesty' only applies to the Queen and the Queen Mother. When being introduced or described they are referred to as: Her Majesty, Queen Elizabeth II, and Her Majesty, Queen Elizabeth, The Queen Mother.

His Royal Highness, Prince Philip, Duke of Edinburgh

'May it please Your Royal Highness, Mr Chairman . . .' etc. This applies to all immediate members of the Royal family; in direct address they should be referred to as: 'Your Royal Highness' the first time, and thereafter as: 'Sir' or 'Ma'am'.

CORRECT FORM

The Peerage

Duke	Your Grace

Marquess	My Lord
Earl	
Viscount	
Baron	

Duchess	Your Grace

Marchioness	Madam or My Lady
Countess	
Viscountess	
Baroness	

Knights

When 'distinguishing' a 'Sir' in the address before a speech, the surname is dropped, e.g. if Sir Harold Wilson were present: 'Sir Harold'.

Heads of Organisations

The head of the organisation or group which is organising the function at which you are speaking should be addressed 'Mr', for example: 'Mr Chairman' or 'Mr President'.

The Church of England

Archbishops of Canterbury and York	Your Grace

Other Archbishops	Your Grace

Retired Archbishop of Canterbury (on retirement a peerage is usually created)	Your Grace, or Lord

Bishop of London	Right Reverend and Right Honourable

or (in subsequent reference)	Bishop
or (if preferred)	My Lord Bishop
Other Bishops of England and Wales	Bishop
or (if preferred)	My Lord or Right Reverend Sir
Bishops of the Church of Scotland	Primus
Bishops of the Church of Ireland	Most Reverend or The Right Reverend
Dean	Dean
Provost	Provost or Mr Provost
Archdeacon	Archdeacon or Mr Archdeacon
Prebendary	Prebendary or Prebendary (followed by surname)
Vicar or Rector	Mr (followed by surname) or Father (followed by surname)
The Right Reverend the Abbot	Father Abbot
The Reverend the Prior	Father Prior
The Reverend Superior-General	Father Superior
The Reverend Mother Superior	Reverend Mother
Chaplains to HMS Forces	Rabbi or Minister or Padre (as the case may be)

CORRECT FORM

Lord High Commissioner to the   Your Grace
General Assembly (Church of
Scotland)

Moderator of the General Assembly   Moderator
(Church of Scotland)

Roman Catholic Church

Pope   Your Holiness

Cardinal   Your Eminence

Archbishop   Your Grace

Bishop   My Lord or The Bishop

Monsignor   Monsignor (followed by surname) or
                Monsignore

Provincial   Father Provincial

Canon   Canon (followed by surname)

The Jewish Community

Chief Rabbi   Chief Rabbi

Rabbi   Rabbi (followed by surname) or
                         Dr (followed by surname) if a
                         doctor

Ministers   Mr (followed by surname) or
                         Dr (followed by surname) if a
                         doctor

The Sephardi Synagogue   The Very Reverend the Haham

CORRECT FORM

Diplomatic

Ambassador	Your Excellency
Minister	Minister or by name
Chargé d'Affaires and acting High Commissioners	Chargé d'Affaires or by name

Civic

Lord Mayor	My Lord Mayor
Lady Mayoress	My Lady Mayoress
Mayor of a City	Mr Mayor
Mayor of a Borough	Mr Mayor
If a Lady Mayor	Madam Mayor
Chairman	Mr Chairman
If untitled lady is Chairman	Madam Chairman

Academic

Chancellor of a University	Mr Chancellor or by his rank or title
Vice-Chancellor of a University	Mr Vice-Chancellor or by rank, title or name

Order of Precedence

Wedding:
Bride and Bridegroom
Host and Hostess

Parents of the Groom
Reverend Sir (or you can follow Reverend with surname; likewise for Rabbi)
Ladies and Gentlemen

In other situations, the chairman is always mentioned first, except when Royalty are present, i.e:
   'May it please Your Majesty, Mr Chairman', and so on, or,
   'May it please Your Royal Highness, Mr Chairman'.
   Sometimes the chairman is also a Lord; he is then referred to as 'My Lord and Chairman' or 'My Lord and President' if the chair is taken by the President of the organisation.

Note: Correct form should be precisely that: *correct*.

When you are invited to speak, you must find out from your host if any titled people are likely to be in the audience. You can then prepare. If you do not have this information until the actual time of the event, then if in doubt of correct form, ask the toastmaster.

Useful Quips
and Quotations

GENERAL ADVICE

If you are unsure of how to introduce quotations into your speech, the following is a simple method:

> When I knew I was going to have to mention sailing/golf/acting/horse-riding/cricket, because that is ———'s great interest, I thought I would look up what great writers and poets of the past have said about sailing . . . The poet ——— said '———'.

If the quotation is a common one you could acknowledge this fact but turn it into a plus. 'We all know the lovely poem by ——— which you can never tire of hearing (Pause) . . .' You could then recite the poem.

If you happen to know the person's tastes you could say:

> I would like to read you just the first verse/line of one of ———'s favourite poems about the sea. It was written by ——— and the title is '———'.

Make all your points positive. Try and relate your subject to his interests, for example, 'I hope he will have many enjoyable voyages/sailing trips in the future.' A similar ploy can be used to illustrate professions or hobbies with original effect.

If your audience includes people who speak different languages or religions, make sure that they can enjoy the quotations too. For example you might say: 'Whatever your religious background, you can appreciate the beautiful poetry of the psalms.'

Here are some quotations which you may find useful for using in your speeches.

Marriage
Marriage is an alliance entered into by a man who can't sleep with the window shut, and a woman who can't sleep with the window open.

George Bernard Shaw

Marriage, the golden rule . . . No woman should marry a teetotaller, or a man who does not smoke.

Robert Louis Stevenson

I belong to Bridegrooms Anonymous. Whenever I feel like getting married, they send over a lady in a house coat and hair curlers to burn my toast for me.

Dick Martin

Marriage, a market which has nothing free but the entrance.

Michel de Montaigne

Before marriage, a man declares that he would lay down his life for you; after marriage, he won't even lay down his newspaper to talk to you.

Helen Rowland

No man should marry until he has studied anatomy and dissected at least one woman.

Honoré de Balzac

The most happy marriage I can picture or imagine to myself would be the union of a deaf man to a blind woman.

Samuel Taylor Coleridge

USEFUL QUIPS AND QUOTATIONS

He married a woman to stop her getting away. Now she's there all day.

Philip Larkin

A man can be a fool and not know it – but not if he is married.

H.L. Mencken

Marriage is a bribe to make the housekeeper think she's a householder.

Thornton Wilder

One wishes marriage for one's daughter and, for one's descendants, better luck.

Fay Weldon

Marriage is an adventure, like going to war.

G.K. Chesterton

When a girl marries she exchanges the attentions of many men for the inattention of one.

Helen Rowland

It has been discovered experimentally that you can draw laughter from an audience anywhere in the world, of any class or race, simply by walking on to a stage and uttering the words: 'I am a married man.'

Ted Kavanagh

When a man marries his mistress it creates a job opportunity.

Sir James Goldsmith

Buy Old Masters. They fetch a better price than old mistresses.

Lord Beaverbrook

Advice for those about to marry. Don't.

Punch, 1845

USEFUL QUIPS AND QUOTATIONS

Husbands
A good husband makes a good wife.

Robert Burton

I began as a passion and ended as a habit, like all husbands.

George Bernard Shaw

Husbands are like fire. They go out if unattended.

Zsa Zsa Gabor

Nothing flatters a man as much as the happiness of his wife; he is always proud of himself as the source of it.

Dr Samuel Johnson

Marrying a man is like buying something you've been admiring in a shop window. You may love it when you get home, but it doesn't always go with everything else in the house.

Jean Kerr

Wives
I think of my wife and I think of Lot and I think of the lucky break he got.

William Cole

Men and Women
Behind every successful man stands a surprised mother-in-law.

Hubert Humphrey

I haven't spoken to my mother-in-law for eighteen months – I don't like to interrupt her.

Ken Dodd

Never go to bed mad, stay up and fight.

Phyllis Diller

Men play the game; women know the score.

Roger Woddis

USEFUL QUIPS AND QUOTATIONS

Why does a woman work ten years to change a man's habits and then complain that he's not the man she married?

Barbra Streisand

Women prefer men who have something tender about them – especially the legal kind.

Kay Ingram

There is a vast difference between the savage and the civilised man, but it is never apparent to their wives until after breakfast.

Helen Rowland

There are two things a real man likes – danger and play; and he likes woman because she is the most dangerous of playthings.

Friedrich Nietzsche

All women become like their mothers. That is their tragedy. No man does. That's his.

Oscar Wilde

Success
Mark Twain bemoaned that he had not seen the Niagara Falls, so they made up a special party to take him there. Afterwards his hosts said, 'What did you think of it?'

Mark Twain paused. 'It's certainly a success,' he said.

Dismissal
The chairman of a large company called in his directors, one by one. Eventually, only the newest and most junior director was left outside the chairman's office. When his turn came, he found his colleagues sitting around a table.

Chairman: 'Bill, have you been having an affair with my secretary, Miss Jones?'

Bill: 'Certainly not.'

'Are you sure?'

'Absolutely. I've never laid a hand on her.'

'Are you absolutely certain?'

'Of course I am.'
'Very well, Steven, then *you* sack her.'

Education
The managing director of a large computer company invited school classes to see round the factory. One of the teachers was overheard at the end of the morning saying to his class: 'There you are, boys and girls. You have now seen where *you* may end up, if you don't do well in your O-levels!'

Business
Everyone lives by selling something.

Robert Louis Stevenson

Nothing is illegal if one hundred businessmen decide to do it.

Andrew Young

There's no such thing as a free lunch.

Milton Friedman

I have always felt that our business men, if they had been left to themselves to make a religion, would have turned out something uncommonly like Juju.

Mary Kingsley

Finance
If you would like to know the value of money, go and try and borrow some.

Benjamin Franklin

We all need money, but there are degrees of desperation.

Anthony Burgess

When I was young I used to think that money was the most important thing in life; now that I am old, I know it is.

Oscar Wilde

USEFUL QUIPS AND QUOTATIONS

Law

The only road to the highest stations in this country is that of the law.

Sir William Jones

Lawyers know life practically. A bookish man should always have them to converse with.

Dr Samuel Johnson

A solicitor is a man who calls in a person he doesn't know to sign a contract he hasn't seen to buy property he doesn't want with money he hasn't got.

Sir Dingwall Bateson, President of the Law Society, 1952–53

I think you may class the lawyer in the natural history of monsters.

John Keats

I really went to the Bar because I thought it would be easier to go on the stage after falling at the Bar than to go to the Bar after falling on the stage.

Lord Gardiner

Ethics

A son asks his father at dinner: 'What are ethics?'

'Leave me alone to eat,' father replies.

'But I must know. I have to write an essay tonight, which I must hand in tomorrow. Ethics is the title.'

'I see. Well, suppose I am closing the shop at night and I find a five pound note on the floor. I check the till and make sure that we are not five pounds light. Then, what do I do? I tell my partner, that's what. And I split it with him. That's ethics.'

Bribery

When we know that one of our customers will not accept the whisky which we send him for Christmas, we send even more the following year – because then we know that it will be sent back and we can drink it ourselves . . .

It's not bribery if you can eat it, drink it or sleep with it.

Jewish Business
Three Jewish men met for dinner.
    The first said 'Oi!'
    The second said 'Oi yevay!'
    The third said: 'If you boys are going to talk business, I'm off . . .'

Accountancy
If someone asks me: 'What is two and two?', I answer:
    'Are you buying or selling?'

Lord Grade

Navy
A sailor never wants to be where he is, but always longs to be where he is not. When a sailor stops complaining the time has come to start worrying.

Prince Charles

Don't talk to me about naval tradition. It's nothing but rum, sodomy and the lash.

Sir Winston Churchill

We are as near to heaven by seas as by land.

Sir Humphrey Gilbert

We sailors get money like horses, and spend it like asses.

Tobias Smollett

Army
Two army captains were grousing about the stupidity of their respective batmen. They decided to have a bet on which one was more stupid. Captain X called for his batman and said: 'Take this five pound note and buy me a colour TV set down in the village.'

'Yes, sir. Certainly, sir.' He saluted and went out into the mess room.

Captain Y then rang for his batman and said: 'Go to the orderly room immediately and see whether I am there'.

'Yes, sir. Certainly, sir.' The batman saluted and left. The two batmen met in the corridor outside and compared notes. 'Fancy asking me to buy a colour TV set on an early closing day,' said the first. The second replied: 'Imagine making me walk half a mile when he could have used the telephone to see if he's in the orderly room!'

He learned the arts of riding, fencing, gunnery,
   And how to scale a fortress – or a nunnery.

Lord Byron

Drinking is the soldier's pleasure.

John Dryden

Medicine
God heals, and the doctor takes the fee.

Benjamin Franklin

Doctors think a lot of patients are cured who have simply quit in disgust.

Don Herold

He wastes no time with patients: and when you have to die, he will finish the business quicker than anybody else.

Molière

Half the modern drugs could well be thrown out of the window, except that the birds might eat them.

Martin Henry Fischer

Vaccination is the medical sacrament corresponding to baptism.
Samuel Butler

USEFUL QUIPS AND QUOTATIONS

Dentistry
The best of friends fall out, and so
  His teeth had done some years ago.

Thomas Hood

When examined by the Divisional Surgeon, defendant was very abusive, and when asked to clench his teeth he took them out, gave them to the doctor and said 'You clench them.'

Police Report – Woking Herald and News

She laughs at everything you say. Why? Because she has fine teeth.

Benjamin Franklin

Hamlet's Advice

Shakespeare wrote great speeches. Hamlet's advice:

Speak the speech, I pray you, as I pronounced it to you, trippingly on the tongue; but if you mouth it, as many of your players do, I had as lief the town crier spoke my lines. Nor do not saw the air too much with your hand, thus; but use all gently: for in the very torrent, tempest, and, as I may say, whirlwind of your passion, you must acquire and beget a temperance that may give it smoothness . . . Be not too tame neither, but let your own discretion be your tutor: suit the action to the word, the word to the action; with this special observance, that you o'erstep not the modesty of nature.

Index

absent friends, toast to 90–91
academic dignitaries
  forms of address 162
address, form of 188–92
after-dinner speeches 10, 117–31
  humour 5–6, 118–19, 122–4
  sample 125–30
  stance 124–5
age, quotations 113
alcohol 57
Androcles 5, 15
anecdotes 15, 118–19, 122
  sources 132
  at weddings 86–7
anniversaries 105–13
  birthdays 106–7, 110–13
  quotations 113
  weddings 105–6; silver 107–10
announcements 156
apologies
  for small audience 159–60
army, jokes about 201–2
Aspel, Michael 60
attention 19, 52
attitude 47
audience 5
  attention 19, 52
  profile 9–11
  rapport 5, 78–9, 175–6
  small 11, 159–60
Autocue 30–31, 73
awards presentation 134–7
  school 135–6
  sporting 142–7

Ball, Tony 121
bar mitzvah 183
behaviour problems 174–5
best man, at wedding 40, 85, 90,
  98, 100–101
birthdays 106–7, 110–13
  21st 112–13
body language 41–7, 51, 52, 61,
  158
booking speakers 161–3
boredom 52, 53
brainstorming 8
breathing 55
brevity 11–12
bride, toast proposed by 100
briefing speakers 149, 161–3
Burns, Robert 15
business speeches
  after-dinner 117–31
  employee getting married
    140–41
  jokes 198–9, 200–201
  retirement 7, 141

cards, speech on 22–3, 29
chairman 149–60
  political meetings 138–9
Chesterton, G.K. 83, 162
children, quotations 116
christenings 114–16
Church of England
  forms of address 189–91
Churchill, Sir Winston 119, 178,
  201

205

INDEX

civic dignitaries
  forms of address 192
close of speech 13, 14, 20–21,
    76–7
club, sports 144–5
coming of age 112–13
committees 149, 151
compèring 157
competitive presentations 185–7
conferences 156
confidence 4–5
contingency plans 158–60
conversation 4
correct form 188–93
Coward, Noel 48, 102, 137
cricket 147
cultures, different 182

delegations, visiting 184
delivery 4, 27, 51, 60–75
dentistry, jokes about 203
dialect 62
  jokes 124
diction 62–5
dinner, hosting 154–5
Dior, Christian 83
Diplomatic forms of address
    192
dismissal, jokes about 198–9
doctors, jokes about 90, 202
Dodds, Michael 21
drafting speech 22–7
dress 48–50, 52
drink 57

editing speech 58–9, 77–8
education
  jokes and quotations 137, 199
  school occasions 135–6
Einstein, Dr Albert 166
elections, political 138–9

emergencies 157–8, 159
empathy and rapport 5, 78–9, 87,
    175
endings, speeches 13, 14, 20–21,
    76–7
energy generator 55–6
entertainment events 157
enthusiasm 1, 3, 4, 47
equipment, setting up 150, 159
  see also slides
examples, giving 19–20
exercises, relaxation and voice
    63–4
expression, facial 45
extemporaneous speaking 178

facts
  file 7, 131–2
  historical 15–16
  research 7, 84, 120
father of the bride 88–9, 92, 93,
    94–6
fear 3, 5–6, 54–7
feedback 15, 51–2, 61–2
Ferber, Edna 82
Fields, W.C. 83
flipcharts 33, 34–5, 38–9
food 57
foreign groups 182
form of address 188–92
Franklin, Benjamin 202, 203
fright 3, 5–6, 54–7
funerals 184–5

gesture 45
golf, jokes about 147
grace 80–81, 154
graduation party 183
Graham, Martha 41
graphology, speaking on 17
groom, wedding 89, 98–100, 101

Guild of Professional
    Toastmasters 121

Hamlet 204
Hancock, Tony 132–3
handouts 18
hands 45–7
Harcourt, Sir William 21
Harding, Gilbert 72
Heath, Sir Edward 148
historical facts 15–16, 132
Hope, Bob 146, 147
horse-riding 147–8
Hubbard, Elbert 149
humour
    in speeches 20, 40, 53, 78, 90;
        after-dinner 5–6, 118–19,
        122–3
    see also anecdotes; jokes
husbands, quotations 197

impromptu speaking 11, 177–8
information 7–8, 20
    historical 15–16
    research 7, 84, 120
interviews 73
introduction
    by chairman 150, 152–3
    by speaker 16–18
Iococca, Lee 2

jargon 12
Jessel, Sir George 54
Jewish business, joke about 201
Jewish Community
    forms of address 191
Johnson, Dr Samuel 58, 103,
    197, 200
jokes
    after-dinner 5–6, 123–4
    army 201–2

bribery 200–201
business 198–9, 200–201
dentistry 203
dismissal 198–9
education 137, 199
ethics 200
finance 199
Jewish business 201
law 200
marriage 195–8
medicine 90, 202
navy 201
success 198
at weddings 90, 195–8

Kanter, Rosabeth Moss 4–5
Kennedy, John F. 137, 138

ladies, toast and reply 81–2
language 12, 27, 77
law, jokes about 200
lectern 28
lectures 178–80
Lennon, John 83
linking 155
literary devices 15
Loyal Toast 80, 155

Mancroft, Lord 161
mannerisms 60–61
marriage
    of employee 140–41
    quotations and jokes 195–8
    second 97–8, 103–4
    see also weddings
master of ceremonies 157
media 72–5
medicine, jokes about 90, 202
meetings, conducting 149–54
men, quotations 83, 197–8
    husbands 104

microphone 69–72
mistakes 132
Montaigne, Michel de 195
municipal elections 139

navy, jokes about 210
nerves and tension 3, 5–6, 54–7
Newbold, Yve 125
newspapers 16, 132
Nietzsche, Friedrich 198
notes 22–3

objectives 8–9
opening, speeches' 13, 14–18, 76
order of precedence 192–3

panel sessions 164
Pankhurst, Christabel 139
Parent–Teacher Associations 9
Parliamentary
  candidates 138
  members, toasting 139
peerage, addressing 189
personality 1, 3
Peters, Tom 51
Phillips, Baroness 122
Philpotts, Eden 142
political speeches 138–9
  quotations 139–40
posture and stance 43–4, 55–6, 63
  after-dinner 124–5
precedence, order of 192–3
preparation, speech 2–3, 7–12,
    13–21, 76–9, 131–2
  drafting 22–7
  immediate 11, 177–8
  on the day 150
  'what if?' list 158–9
presentations 33
  competitive 185–7
prize-giving 134–7

problem behaviour 174–5
professional speakers 2–3
  briefing 162–3
  selecting 161
projector 36–7, 159
pronunciation 66–8

questions 18, 20, 164–76
  question time 12, 165
quips see jokes
quotations 1, 15, 32, 35, 194–203
  age 113
  anniversaries 113
  children 116
  introducing 194–5
  men 83, 104, 197–8
  politics 139–40
  schools 137, 199
  speech-making 1, 204
  sports 146–8
  weddings 84, 102–4, 195–8
  women 82–3, 104, 197–8

radio 74–5
Raphael, Bette-Jane 83
reading others' speeches 26–7
reading style 27–8
rehearsal 58–9, 60–61
relaxation exercises 64–5
research 7, 84, 120
retirement speeches 7, 141
Roman Catholic Church
  forms of address 191
room 10–11, 149–50
Royalty, addressing 188
Rudner, Rita 83

sailing 148
schools 135–7
  quotations and jokes 137, 199
script of speech 22–31, 77

INDEX

seating arrangements 150
second marriages
quotations 103–4
toasts 97–8
sentence length 12, 23, 25
Shakespeare, William 204
Shaw, George Bernard 1, 32, 50, 103, 169, 195, 197
Silver Wedding 107–10
simplicity 11–12
sincerity 3–4
slides 20, 25–6
for lectures 179–80
overhead 33–4, 37–8, 159
projector 36–7, 159
35mm 35–6
speakers
booking 161–2
briefing 162–3
introducing 150, 152–3
welcoming 150
speech-writers 26
sporting toasts 142–6
quotations 146–8
stance and posture 43–4, 55–6, 63,
after-dinner 124–5
Stanners, Edward 125–30
statistics 19, 132
Stevenson, Robert Louis 18, 103, 195, 199
stories 118–19, 122
see also anecdotes; jokes
structure, speech 13–21, 59
style 1–2, 4, 50–53
summary 20–21

Taylor, Elizabeth 83
technical presentation 181
teleprompter 30–31, 73
television 2, 5, 13, 72–4

tension and nerves 3, 5–6, 54–7
text layout 23–5
thanks, vote of 150, 153–4
Thatcher, Lady Margaret 81, 82, 140, 165
theatre 157–8, 169
timing
events 151, 162–3
questions 170
speeches 12, 58
wedding speeches 58, 86
toastmaster 154, 155
Toastmasters, Guild of 121
toasts
absent friends 90–91
birthdays 110–12
ladies 81–2
Loyal 80
M.P.S. 139
quotations 82–3
replies: birthday 110–11, 112, 113; ladies 82; silver wedding 108, 109–10; wedding 98–9, 101
school 136–7
silver wedding 107–10
sporting 142–7
twenty-first birthday 112
wedding 90–101
topic, breaking down 17
training 131
Twain, Mark 177, 198

Ustinov, Sir Peter 53, 121

video, seeing oneself on 15, 60–61
visiting delegations 184

209

INDEX

visual aids 19, 25–6, 32–40
  for lectures 179–80
  see also flipcharts; projector;
    slides
voice 27, 42, 60–64
  delivery 51, 60–75
  exercise 63–4
  modulation 63
  projection 63–4
vote of thanks 150, 153–4

water, drinks 57
wedding anniversary 105–6
  silver 107–10
weddings 4, 10, 11, 40, 84–101
  order of precedence 192–3

quotations and jokes 102–4,
  195–8
  second 97–8, 103–4
  timing of speeches 58, 86
  toasts 89, 90–101
Welles, Orson 82
West, Mae 72, 83, 102
'what if?' list 158–60
Whitehorn, Katharine 83
Wilde, Oscar 140, 198, 199
wives, quotations 104
women
  quotations and jokes 82–3,
    197–8
  toasts 81–2
  wives 104